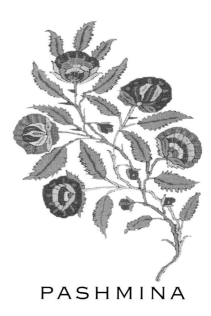

PASHMINA

India Crest

ISBN: 81-7436-239-8

© **Roli & Janssen BV 2003**
Published in India by
Roli Books in arrangement with Roli & Janssen BV
M-75, G. K. II Market, New Delhi-110 048, India.
Phones: (011) 2921 2271, 2921 2782, Fax: (011) 2921 7185
Email: roli@vsnl.com, Website: rolibooks.com

Printed and bound at Singapore

Lustre Press
Roli Books

PASHMINA

~

ANAMIKA PATHAK

Dedicated to my father
Late (Dr) V.P. Dwivedi

ACKNOWLEDGEMENTS

~

I am grateful to Dr Ashok K. Das, Prof of Arts, Santiniketan; Dr Yashodhara Agrawal, Deputy Keeper, Bharat Kala Bhawan; Dr Anand Krishan and Dr Naval Krishan of Benares; from the National Museum: Director General Dr R.D. Choudhury, Assistant Director U. Das, former Keeper Ms Krishna Lal, Curator Dr Daljeet, senior librarian and information officer Mrs Pratibha Parasar, Ms Rima, Ms Tripathi, Mr S.R. Chaube, photographic officer Mr J.C. Arora, senior photographer Mr Tejbir; Mr Donald C. Johnson at the Ames Library of South Asia, Minneapolis. I also thank my companion, Mr S.K. Pathak, mother Urmila Dwivedi, and children Neelabh, Anvita and Sandeep, for their patience and support. A special thanks to Roli Books for giving me the opportunity to write the book.

The author and publisher are thankful to Dr Deborah Swallow, Curator, Victoria and Albert Museum, London; Dr V.N. Singh, Director, Chandigarh Museum; and the National Museum, New Delhi, for giving permission to publish photographs and transparencies from their museum collections.

CONTENTS

7
The Historical Wrap: Woollens Since the Ages

27
Materials and Methods: Making the Shawl

35
Designs on the Loom: The Kanikar Style

63
Wrapped in Shawl

101
Embroidering Magic: Amlikar Artistry

137
Appendix: Woollen Costumes & Jamawar

141
Glossary

143
Bibliography

THE HISTORICAL WRAP:
WOOLLENS SINCE THE AGES

The past few decades have witnessed a spurt of interest in antique Kashmiri shawls among research scholars and art collectors in India and abroad. The complexity of the shawl tradition in India is also a fascinating subject for museums and art collectors who vie to possess these elegantly created shawls, which were a worldwide passion between the eighteenth and nineteenth centuries.

The word shawl is derived from the Indo-Persian word *shal*, which meant a fine woven woollen fabric used as a drape. The Italian traveller Pietro della Valle, in 1623, observed that whereas in Persia the *scial* or shawl was worn as a girdle, in India it was more usually carried 'across the shoulders'. The *shal*, shawl or *do-shalla* (the Hindi term for shawl) has a long history. Although its origins are popularly traced to the medieval period, archaeological findings, ancient literary references, and travellers' accounts provide ample evidence of the existence of the woollen

FACING PAGE: DETAIL OF SHAWL, KASHMIR, C. 1870, 350 X 144 CM

tradition in India right from the Indus Civilization (2700–2000 B.C.).

ARCHAEOLOGICAL EVIDENCE

Sheep and goats are the major sources for obtaining wool, animal fleece or hair, the raw material for making woollen fabrics. Although no woollen yarn has been found so far from any of the excavated sites of the Indus Civilization, there are some important indirect references to wool that indicate the Harappans were as familiar with the use of wool as they were with cotton and silk yarn. Excavated findings of small terracotta figures of goat and sheep from different Indus sites indicate that these animals were domesticated during that period for meat, dairy products and wool. Fragments of cotton, silk and impressions of weave on terracotta potshard clearly show that advanced weaving techniques were prevalent in the Harappan period.

The excavation of dyeing areas in Harappa and Rakhigarhi points to how advanced the decoration of textiles was. The geometric and floral motifs on utensils, pottery, and potsherds reflect the Harappans'

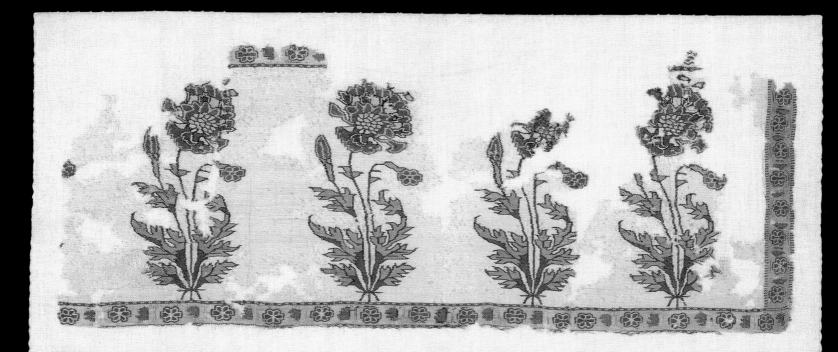

love for ornamentation. These references clearly show that a rich tradition of textiles existed during the Harappan period.

Apart from archaeological evidence within India itself, significant findings of Indian wool outside India came to light in the last century. These findings indicate that Indian wool was so popular for its high quality between A.D. 300 and 400 that it was exported to different countries. Three most important specimens of fragmentary Indian woollen textiles were found from different sites: two from Palmyra, Syria, and one from Antinoe, Egypt. Palmyra was a major Roman outpost on the Silk Road and Antinoe was close to the great urban centre of Alexandria. All these fragments were identified as made from Kashmir wool. Close examination revealed they were produced with the same type of four-ended twills used to produce shawls in Kashmir. The Antinoe specimen seemed identical to the standard type of three-end twills, while the Palmyra specimen appeared even finer and denser, having four-end twills. The Swedish textile authority, Ages Geijer, has commented that the woollen fragments from Palmyra appear to be of Syrian origin, although the wool was from Kashmir. The author has also added that for centuries Syria had been a great meeting point of the textile technology of the East and the West and had access to first-class wool of all kinds, including prized Kashmiri wool, of which the two Palmyra specimens were made.

Riding coats of oriental cut, embellished with patterned silk fabrics of Sassanian manufacture, were found in the excavated sites of Antinoe in 1898. This was another significant discovery in the field of Indian woollen textiles. From the fine material and pattern it appeared that these elegant caftans had been imported readymade from the Sassanian Empire some time between A.D. 300 and 500. The main material of these coats consisted of a thin warp and a thick weft of soft, loosely spun Kashmir wool.

Another important reference to Kashmir wool is of Indian shawls, which were among the several gift items given by Sassanian King Bahram I (r.c. 273 – 276) to Roman Emperor Aurelian (r.c. 270 – 275) after the fall of Palmyra. These references indicate that high-quality Indian textiles were in vogue with the Sassanian elite and were valued highly. The weaving technique was quite close to the Kashmiri tradition. During this period, the Sassanians had close ties with the Yuezhi, a Central Asian nomadic people of Turkish origin who spoke a Persian dialect. They were better

PAGE 8: SHAWL BORDER, KASHMIR, LATE 17TH CENTURY, PASHMINA.
PAGE 9: FRAGMENT OF SHAWL, KASHMIR, 18TH CENTURY, PASHMINA, 15 X 20 CM.
LEFT: WOMAN SPINNING SHAWL WOOL, KASHMIR.

known by their Indian name, the Kushans, and ruled in present-day Kashmir from the late first century B.C. to the third century A.D. This period was considered good for trade plying on the Silk Road between China and Rome. Some sources have included Kashmir wool, perhaps pashmina, among the Indian luxury goods arriving in the Roman Empire via the Silk Road.

ANCIENT LITERARY EVIDENCE

Apart from archaeological excavations in and outside India, the Vedic texts, epics, and Buddhist, Jain and other religious literature also spoke of a tradition of woollen fabrics that existed in India since time immemorial. Vedic literature provides insight into the source of wool, its quality, quantity and the terminology used for wool or woollen fabrics from c.1500 to 800 B.C.E.. The *Rig Veda* and the *Atharva Veda* often mention *Avika* or *Avi*, terms used for sheep during that period. The Vedic dictionary mentions that the person who possesses a sheep is *Avimant*. The *Rig Veda* calls the

AN IMPORTANT FIND

The woollen tradition existed in India right since the Indus Civilization. Excavations at Mohenjodaro, or Mound of the Dead, now in Pakistan, found a stone bust of a bearded priest. This sandstone bust depicts a priest covering his left shoulder with a shawl or mantle. The remarkable fact is that even today Indian men wear shawls in a similar manner. This drape is beautifully ornamented with a slightly raised trefoil pattern arranged in a systematic manner on the entire field of the shawl, which indicates that the fabric must have been woven evenly. Impressions of tiny holes at the corners of the trefoil pattern of each motif reflect embroidery or appliqué work. Embroidery on woollen fabrics is still practised in Kashmir and appliqué temple hangings or banners on felt cloth are still made in Karnataka in South India.

valley of Sindh *suvasa urnavati* because sheep's wool and cloth were available there in plenty. Both the *Rig Veda* and *Atharva Veda* mention that the sheep of Gandhara were famous for the quality of their wool. The area around the Ravi River was noted for its washed or coloured woollen fabrics. The *Atharva Veda* talks of *Kambal*, the generic term for blankets and shawls. The *Yajur Veda* and *Shri Shukul Yajur Veda Satapaltra Brahmana* provide the important reference that during sacrifices, kings were allowed to wear the *pandva*, a kind of woollen fabric. The *Brihadaranyaka Upanishad* says that the *pandvaika*, a kind of woollen fabric, possibly a woollen *chadar* or a shawl, was made from sheep's wool.

The *Taittiriya Samhita* is more specific about terminology and uses *Avi* for female sheep, *Urna-yu* for woollen fabric, and *Urna-vant* for a place abounding in wool. In the *Satapatha Brahmana*, the word *Pushan* was used for 'the Lord of Cattle.' Some interesting references are found in the great epics, Ramayana and Mahabharata, fourth century B.C.E. – fourth century. According to the *Sabha parva* chapter in the Mahabharata, the Pandava king Yudhishtra received several gifts at the time

11

SHAWL, EARLY 19TH CENTURY, PASHMINA.

of the *Rajasuya* yajna from contemporary rulers. The most noteworthy were *rankava* woollen fabrics from the Sakas, who controlled Kashmir during that period, and soft and dyed woollen fabrics made of sheep wool and goat hair from Bactria and also from China. From Kamboja, Yudhishtra received woollen cloth made from sheep's wool and the hair of *vrsadamsa* embroidered with gold, woollen *chadars, pravara* and costly shawls or *kambal*. The Mahabharata informs that during this period felts were made from goat hair *rankava-kata*.

The *Jataka*, stories of Lord Buddha's previous births, also mention the quality of woollen shawls, their colours, and their specific terminology. The *Mahavanija Jataka* provides a list of precious items among which costly shawls from Uddiyan, modern

12

HOW TO WEAR A THREAD

The *Manusmriti*, an ancient code of law, talks about the different uses of wool prevalent in the fourth and fifth centuries. Till that time, wool was known as *Avi* and was used for clothing and to make the sacred thread for the *Yajnopavita* or thread ceremony. The *Yajnopavita* is observed till today, but only by male Brahmans. It involves wearing a sacred thread over the left shoulder. At the time of the ancient lawgiver Manu, it was also practised by other *varnas* or classes. The only difference was in the types of material used. For example, the *Manusmriti* mentions that the *Vaishya varna or* the traders were supposed to wear the *avika* or wool thread It informs that *ritha* was used for washing the wool thead to give a shine to the woollen garments. The practice continues even today.

KASHMIR WOMAN CARDING PASHM (SHAWL WOOL), SKETCH OF J.L. KIPLING, AMRITSAR, 1870.

Swat, are mentioned. At the beginning of the last century, when Sir Aural Stein visited the Swat valley, he found women weaving Swati *kambals* with bright red borders. The *Sivi Jataka* mentions that a shawl, around a hundred thousand *karsapanas,* was presented to the King of Kosala. The *Vessantara Jataka* talks of the *pandu kambal,* a yellow blanket, and the *Sasa Jataka* mentions that Indra's throne was covered with the *pandu kambal,* the best variety of wool. The *Mahavastu* mentions a guild of weavers. At the same time, new terms came up. The terms *kambal* and *rankavas* became more popular for *dushala, chadar,* and other woollen fabrics. In Punjabi and Hindi, *dussa* even today means a rough woollen *chadar.* The literature of the Buddhist period suggests these shawls were expensive. From Sanskrit and Pali sources, we know that *rankava* was the generic name for woollen goods and was derived from *ranku.* A few writers had identified it as a type of wild goat, perhaps the Himalayan ibex, while others believed it was the Tibetan pashm goat *(Capra sibirica).* There was also a great demand for ordinary blankets and camel rugs, which shows the popularity of woollen items apart from that of woollen fabrics.

The Jain text, *Nisithacurni,* mentions that shawls made of goats' hair were used between the sixth and fifth century B.C. Panini's famous text of the fifth century B.C. mentions that in the northwest frontiers of the country, the term *brithatika* was commonly used for wool, and *pravara* for *kambal,* which was made of the fleece of wild animals. *Kambal* was perhaps derived from *kamblya*—a weight. Kashika, a commentary on Panini's *Ashtadhyayi,* informs that five seers of wool

13

made a *kamblya* and the fabric thus made was called *kambal*. Writer V. S. Agrawala holds that it was a thin and finer quality of *kambal*, something like *tus* or *dushala*, which later became a general term for any wool wrapper.

Avi, avika, rankava, kambal, and *paravara* were the terms used for woollen fabrics in the Epic, Vedic, Buddhist, Hindu, and Jain periods. During the Mauryan period, from the third to second century B.C., several changes occurred. The most significant written record of that time is Kautilya's *Arthasastra,* which mentions that woollen fabrics, *avika,* had various colours: *suddha* or white, *suddharakta* or red, and *paksa rakta,* half red and half white. If *rakta* derived from *ranj* means dyed, the three terms may also mean un-dyed, fully dyed, and partially dyed. This text also talks of the different categories of fabric/shawls available—the *Khacita, Vanacitra, Khandasamghatya,* and *Tantuvicchinna,* which translate as follows:

Khacita seems to imply some sort of knitting. According to Dr Moti Chandra, this shawl could either be made by weaving and embroidering or by the twill tapestry technique that would involve making the *Khacita* shawls by both the woven, or *tilakar,* and embroidered, or *amlikar,* processes. The next type of shawl referred to in the text is *Vancita.* For it, designs were woven on the loom as in the modern *tilakar* technique. The third category is the *Khandasamghatya,* which is described as a shawl made by joining many *Khacita* or woven pieces. These strips were either woven or embroidered. The last category is *Tantuvicchinna,* which embodies net or lace work. Apart from these four varieties, there were different types of woollen textiles also—animal coverings, carpets, caps, blankets, and *chadar.* The Mauryans valued quality craftsmanship. To maintain standards in art, Kautilya advised penalising artisans who did not discharge their duties. Weavers, dyers, tailors, and washers were among the list of artisans mentioned. These references point to the fact that during the Mauryan period, a tradition of woollen fabrics not only existed but also had an important place in society.

The next important work is *Amarakosa,* which talks of the *rallaka,* a woollen shawl of the fourth century A.D. The *rallakas* were made from the soft animal hair of the *ranku,* a species of deer or antelope. The *rallaka* was the equivalent of the modern pashmina and was costly. Since it was a high quality fabric, it was often used as a tribute gift.

The literature of the Gupta period, especially the sixth-century copperplate inscription of Vijayasen, is very significant in the context of woollen fabrics. Written in the Brahmi script and in Sanskrit, it was found at Mallasarul in Burdwan district, West Bengal, and belongs to the time of Gopa Chandra (regnal year 33). This too uses *urna* to refer to wool. The owner or a superintendent of a wool market or a wool factory is known as an *urnasthanik.* After the Gupta and later Gupta periods, the literature of Kashmir and of the Sultanate period provides some evidence of wool.

EVIDENCE OF MEDIEVAL LITERATURE

There are more references to Indian woollen clothing in the medieval period than in the ancient period. The medieval period witnessed the zenith of the Kashmir shawl industry as it received royal patronage, had royal *karkhanas,* or workshops, and benefited from the ruler's personal supervision. With the result, fine woollen clothing was created and new experiments were made. Slowly the fame of the Kashmir shawl spread and English and French weavers began imitating it.

However, there is no unanimity over when the Kashmir shawl industry started. There are two different views. Scholars John Irwin (1952) and Frank

EMPEROR OF FASHION

Mughal Emperor Akbar (1526-1605), famous as an empire builder, also began a new style in wearing shawls. According to the *Ain-i-Akbari*, a document of his time and life, he introduced the practice of *do-shalla*, wearing of two shawls back-to-back so that the reverse side was not visible. Akbar himself possessed many Kashmiri shawls and took a keen interest in the industry. He set up imperial *karkhanas* or workshops at Lahore (Punjab), Agra, Fatehpur (Uttar Pradesh), and Ahmedabad (Gujarat) to manufacture excellent fabrics. Also, several changes were made in the style, fabric, dyeing, and pattern of textiles. Apart from the variety of fabrics made in the workhop or *karkhana*, the *Ain-i-Akbari* gives information about how the emperor wore the shawl and the method of storage. Akbar's encouragement to indigenous workers and good judgment about the trade led to an all-round improvement. Thus, demand for the fine material increased, which for the first time invited a grand display of draperies. Akbar gave his own Hindi designation, *paramnaram* (very soft) for the generic term *sal*, and he changed the name of *Kapurdhur* (camphor dust), a Tibetan item, to *kapurnur* (camphor light).

Ames (1980) are of the opinion that Sultan Zain-ul-Abidin (1420 – 70) of Kashmir founded the industry in Kashmir, importing weavers from Andijan in Russian Turkistan and bringing about innovations. These weavers introduced the twill tapestry weave and other major techniques used in shawl production. This type of weaving found a parallel in Persia and Central Asia, but nowhere in the Indo-Pakistan subcontinent. To support their view, scholars cite Srivara Pandit's *Jaina Rajtarangini,* where Zain-ul-Abidin is praised for promoting the craft of shawl weaving.

Scholars Moti Chandra (1954), Chandramani Singh, and Devaki Ahivasi (1981) hold that the industry existed earlier than the fifteenth century. The eleventh-century author, Kshemendra (990 – 1065), gives important clues about the antiquity of the twill tapestry technique. In his work, *Desopadesa*, he refers to *tusta-pravarana*, which seems to be a variety of woollen fabric. In *Narmamala*, he speaks of the *paryanta-tustaka*, an inferior variety of shawl with borders. He also narrates how a teacher employed in a Kayastha house for children, spent his time spinning *kartana*, drawing out *likhanam* and weaving patterns on the strips with *tujis* or eyeless wooden needles—the process, *sucipattkavanam,* being analogous to modern shawl weaving in Kashmir. These references make it clear that shawl weaving was practised in Kashmir around the eleventh century. Like any other industry, the shawl industry also developed in phases and took shape in due course, which could be around the time of Zain-ul-Abidin. This conjecture is supported by a popular Kashmiri story. The references also make it clear that shawl weaving was connected not only with Kashmir, but flourished in many other places such as Swat, North Western Frontier Province, Punjab, and other places.

During Alauddin's reign (1296 – 1316), according to the *Sarur-us-sudu*, a thirteenth-fourteenth century text, shawls were available and considered prized possessions in Delhi. Sheikh Nizamuddin Auliya had one such shawl. *Dharmabhyudaya*, the thirteenth-century manuscript written by Udayaprabha Suri, mentions that woollen goods reached Western India from Kashmir and Kashmiri shawls, *Kasmiravasana,* were used, especially at the time of worship in the sanghas and *caityas*.

The fifteenth-century *Jaina Rajtarangini* gives a detailed account of the life and culture of Kashmir. Sultan Zain-ul-Abidin, the Akbar of Kashmir, ruled the Valley and his interest in textiles led to a flourishing industry. During his reign, woollen goods that came from distant lands began to be manufactured in Kashmir. The Sultan's interest was in patterns, *citra,* and creeper designs, *latakritih*. The creeper designs were obtained by an intricate weaving process known as *vicitravayana*. The text further mentions that rulers sent the Sultan special textiles of their regions as gifts. Rajput rulers sent printed cloths or *narikunjara*. Sultan Mahmud Beghra (1458 – 1511) sent different clothes such as *katepha, saglata*, and *sopha*. These clothes could also be identified with *qatif*, a silken stuff; *saqlat,* a broad scarlet cloth; and *suf* or woollen cloth—these terms are mentioned in the *Ain-i-Akbari*.

Akbar was the next significant ruler to give attention to wool making. Abul Fazal's *Ain-i-Akbari* discussed in detail Akbar's initiative towards establishing the shawl and textile industry. The *Ain-i-Akbari* enumerates four areas—the material, the colour, the manufacture, and the dress material—in which Akbar improved the shawl:

'The improvement is visible first in *tus* shawls, which are made of the wool of an animal of that name whose natural colour is black, white and red but chiefly black; sometimes the colour is pure white. This kind of shawl is unrivalled for its lightness, warmth, and softness. People generally wear it without altering its natural colour and His Majesty has had it dyed. It is curious that it will not take red dye. [According to this text, the *tus* shawl was made from the hair of the *tus* goat.]

[The second improvement is found in] 'the *safid alcas*, any kind of coloured stuff or *tarahadars* in their

TWO MEN IN CONVERSATION. THE YELLOW SHAWL IS IMPORTANT IN THE ATTIRE, COMPANY SCHOOL, 19TH CENTURY.

natural colours, their wool being white, black or mixed. The white kind was formerly dyed in three or four ways. His Majesty has given orders to dye it in various ways. During this period the corded and patterned or *tarah* shawls were made of white, black or mixed wool.

'The third group relates to various techniques of ornamenting the *zardozi* shawls embroidered with

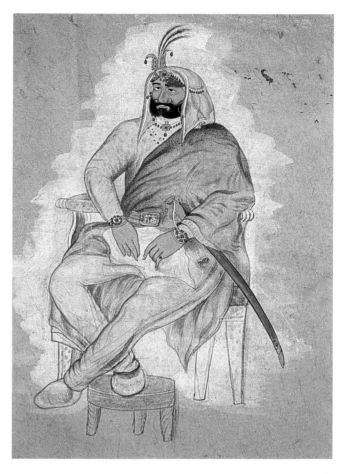

THE SHAWL IS A PROMINENT PART OF THE GARMENTS OF A SIKH COUPLE, SIKH PERIOD, 19TH CENTURY.

PORTRAIT OF MAHARAJA SHER SINGH IN A PINK SHAWL. IT SHOWS THE POPULARITY OF THE SHAWL. SIKH PERIOD, 19TH CENTURY.

gold wire and sequins, or with *kalbatun* (the design seemed to have been brocaded with gold wire), *qasidah* (the pattern was embroidered), *qalghai* (made either of silk or gold wire or with pinecone patterns), *banghnun* (shawls with typed pattern), *chint* (shawls painted or decorated with floral patterns in the manner of calico prints), *alcah* (a white-banded item), and *purzdar* (a shawl obtained by joining together several stripes, the *khandasamghatya* of ancient times), to which his Majesty pays much attention.

'Lastly an improvement was made in the width. His Majesty had the pieces made large enough to yield the making of a full dress.'

It appears that Akbar not only took an interest in shawl making, but also in dress materials. With more than a thousand workshops, Jahore (Lahore) became

KRISHNA AND RADHA STANDING UNDER AN UMBRELLA. KRISHNA IS WEARING A WOOLLEN BLACK CLOAK/SHAWL ON HIS SHOULDER, KANGRA, 18TH CENTURY.

century memoir of Jahangir (1605 – 1628), has several references to textiles. It talks about the shawl's material, manufacturing, pattern, and the raw material. 'The wool for the shawls comes from a goat which is peculiar to Tibet,' it informs. At one place, it says, 'The shawls of Kashmir to which my father gave the name of *paramnaram* are very famous: there is no need to praise them. Another kind is *taharma*, which is thicker than a shawl and soft.' *Naharama* is another name used in the text. It means 'like a river', probably on account of the shawl having a wavy pattern. *Darm* is another form of shawl that like a *jul-i-khirsak* is put on the floor as a carpet. The *Tuzuk-i-Jahangiri* also refers to a special *phup* shawl, which Jahangir once presented to Mirza Raja Bhao Singh. According to Dr Chandra, *phup* stands for the Hindi word *pushpa* derived from the Sanskrit *puspa*, meaning flower. The *tus* shawl, notes the memoir, was the king's prerogative: only those who were given it could wear it.

The shawl industry did well during the reigns of Shahjahan (1628 – 1658) and his son Aurangzeb (1658 – 1707). The design and the colour combination received more attention. The demand was high and increase in production created a good market within and outside India. Better availability of *tus* shawls also points to the fact that they had ceased to be a royal monopoly.

The *Khulasat-ut-Tawarikh* (1695) mentions that around the last quarter of the seventeenth century, different types of shawls were manufactured in Kashmir and exported. As a result the shawls had achieved widespread fame, not only in Kashmir or *Kashmiria*, but also in Europe. The *Kalpadrukosa* of Kesava, a seventeenth-century Sanskrit lexicon, gives some interesting names for shawl: *ratnakambal, kasmiri, mahorna, pravari, pamari, yaksika* and *bhota*. *Kasmiri* and *bhota* were the products of Kashmir and Tibet respectively. *Ratnakambal* must have been a

a centre of shawl weaving and produced *mayan* that was used for turbans and waistbands.

Akbar's son, Jahangir, was also interested in the shawl industry, which flourished well in his region. The famous text *Tuzuk-i-Jahangiri*, the seventeenth-

costly shawl, *pravari* a *chadar*, and *pamari* a foot spread.

Emperor Muhammad Shah (1720 – 48) was also fond of Kashmiri shawls. He used to buy shawls with a particular floral pattern every year that cost Rs 40,000. Kashmir weavers named this pattern *Buta Muhammad Shahi*. But only weavers remember the name. The form of the motif has changed and it is hard to say today what it originally looked like.

The Afghans ruled Kashmir after the Mughals and they took a keen interest in the shawl trade. Shawls and other woollen clothing manufactured during this period can be distinguished by several changes in pattern, design, and colour. The square or moon shawls, which became very popular in the Far East, Turkey, and Russia and the European markets, were their main contribution.

The Sikhs occupied Kashmir after the Afghan rulers in 1819 and ruled for a few decades. The French, British, and other Europeans visited the Sikh court and their descriptive accounts regarding courtly decoration with textiles are a valuable source of information. These descriptions and the miniature paintings of the Sikh period point to the importance of shawl and its multi-purpose use. One such painting in the British museum, *The Death of Ranjeet Singh,* is quite interesting in this context. It shows the passion Maharaja Ranjeet Singh had for shawls. The painted death scene depicts three different shawls. The ruler lies on his deathbed over a yellow shawl, his body covered by a maroon shawl with a 'folded, stripped *khatraz* or *jamawar* type shawl' placed near his head.

According to literary sources, Maharaja Ranjeet Singh had also commissioned a pair of shawls depicting his victories. However, according to G.T. Vigne, only one pair was completed, but its whereabouts are not known. During this period long and *do-shalla* shawls became popular and were made with new motifs.

The Dogra rulers came after the Sikhs in Kashmir. Their contribution was in the field of embroidered shawls. During this period, the size, design, pattern, colour and the technique of making shawls changed. Magnificent embroidered shawls were made colourful, and a few noteworthy shawls were the *do-rukha,* embroidered on both sides, and the long, rectangular shawls. One such shawl—a magnificent example housed in the Chandigarh museum—commissioned by Gulab Singh of Jammu illustrates scenes from the *Sikandarnama.* Around 1870, Maharaja Ranbir Singh commissioned the 'map shawls', which etch a bird's eye perspective of Srinagar and the Kashmir valley. Four such shawls have been found so far.

The Kashmir shawl industry flourished under royal patronage whether it was from the Kashmiris, Mughals, Afghanis, Sikhs, or Dogras. Around the last quarter of the eighteenth century, the shawl's fame drew English and French weavers to imitate it. Kashmir-like shawls began to be produced in Norwich in England, Paisley in Scotland, and France.

TRAVELLERS' ACCOUNTS

Around 596 - 664, the famous Chinese pilgrim Xuanzang visited India. While describing Indian dresses, he made important references to goat hair costumes: 'They have garments also of *Ts'o-mo kshauma*, which is a sort of hemp garment also made of *Kien-po-lo kambal*, which is woven with fine goat hair. Garments are also made from *Ho-la-li karala*. This stuff is made from the fine hair of a wild animal: it is seldom that this can be woven, and therefore the stuff is very valuable and is regarded as fine clothing.'

During the fourteenth century, Ibn Batuta came to India from Arabia. Ibn Batuta describes a very important gift exchange that took place in 1342

SIKH CLERGY WEARING SHAWLS. LATE 19TH CENTURY.
FOLLOWING PAGES 22-23: SHAWL, KASHMIR, C.1870,
PASHMINA, 350 X 144 CM.

between Emperor Shun (r.1333 – 68) of the Yuan dynasty (1279 – 1368) and Muhammad bin Tughlaq (r.1325 – 51), the Sultan of Delhi. The Chinese ruler sent costly silks and jewel-studded garments to the Sultan who, in exchange, sent five cotton garments, silk dyed in five colours, two hundred additional garments of various fabrics and 'five hundred of goat hair *mar'izz*, of which a hundred were black, green, red

and blue respectively'. The Arabic term *mar'izz* or *mir'izza* means 'fine goat's fleece.'

The next important visitor was Bernier, Aurangzeb's physician. He visited Kashmir in 1655 and left a detailed account of shawl manufacturing. Bernier identified two types of wool: the first obtained from Tibetan goats for making fine shawls; the second from Kashmir. He also mentioned that a few thousand looms produced shawls in Kashmir, generating employment. The mass production is significant: it indicates that by this time the shawl was in popular use. The Mughals prized the shawls that often formed

20

the *khi'lat,* the robe of honour—the complete outfit the Emperor gave to ambassadors or loyal people. In one such ceremony in 1831, a young man 'received four or five dresses of honour, made of thick Benares gold and silver *kimkhwab* or *kinkhab,* which were all put upon his person. And over all these dresses of honour were placed four or five pairs of Cashmere shawls.' The other centres of shawl weaving were Patna, Agra, and Lahore, but fine quality work was the trademark of Kashmir.

Forster, a Frenchman, visited Kashmir in 1783. The wool then, according to him, was brought from Tibet, was usually dark grey, and woven with rich floral patterns. The flowered shawl, which came with new designs, was considerably costlier as compared to plain shawls. According to Forster, shawls were an important export item, so much so that he gave detailed descriptions about their packing, mentioning that a portion of the revenue earned through their sale was sent back to the Afghan capital.

Around the end of the eighteenth century, Kashmir shawls were made in three sizes—long, narrow, and square. Forster further states that square shawls were common in the Indian market. Long and very narrow shawls with black colour schemes were especially made for the Northern Asiatic market, where they were used as girdles.

Moorcroft, who visited India in the early nineteenth century in Kashmir, gave an elaborate description of shawl manufacturing in Kashmir and Amritsar. By that time several changes had occurred. The most noteworthy centre became Amritsar, impressing Moorcroft a lot. He observed that the red shawl yarn used in Amritsar usually came from Kashmir, but its export was banned to discourage the foreign manufacture of shawls. However, Moorcroft noticed that now the wool came from Tibet, Bokhara, and Uzbegestan to Amritsar and shawls were woven with a double warp and weft, giving a fairly thick and soft texture to the fabric. Moorcroft gives a full account of cleaning, spinning, dyeing, weaving, work distribution, weaving techniques, types of shawls, woollen products, fabrics, important technical terms, pricing, trade with different countries and several other minutiae.

Visitors from England and France who visited the court of Maharaja Ranjeet Singh in the nineteenth century appreciated its shawl decoration. A British

WRITERS ON SHAWL FROM 7TH TO 17TH CENTURY

- The Chinese pilgrim Xuanzang, who stayed in India from A.D. 596 to 664, was the first foreigner to write about shawls. He visited India during the early half of the seventh century. He called the *kambal* by the exotic sounding word, *Kein-po-lo.*
- Seven hundred years later came Ibn Batuta from Arabia. He wrote of a gift exchange involving shawls between emperor Shun of the Yuan dynasty and Muhammad bin Tughlaq, the Sultan of Delhi. He used *mar'izz* to mean fine goat's fleece.
- Bernier came during the 17 century. Thanks to him, we know that mass production of shawls had begun in Kashmir at that time.

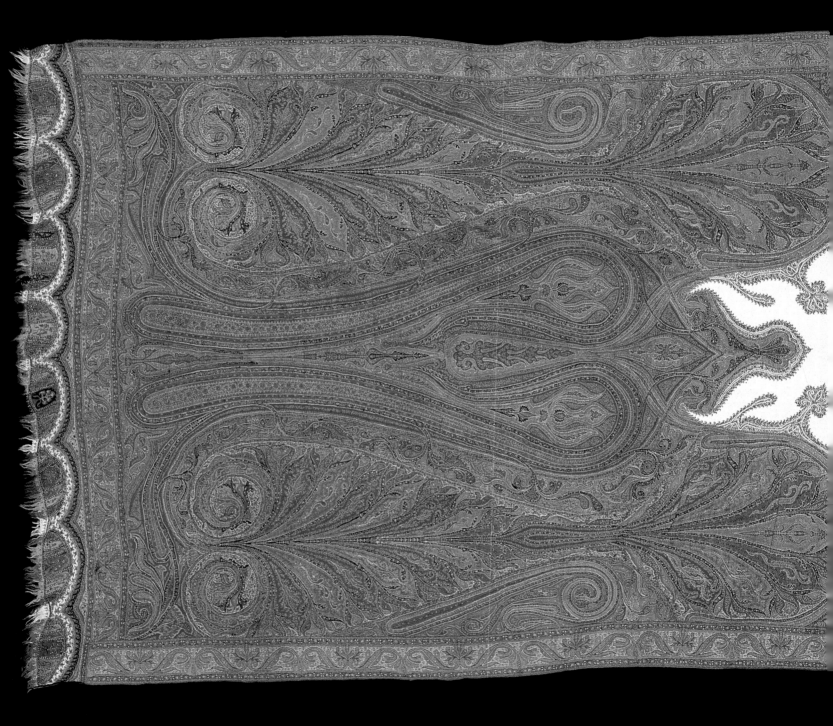

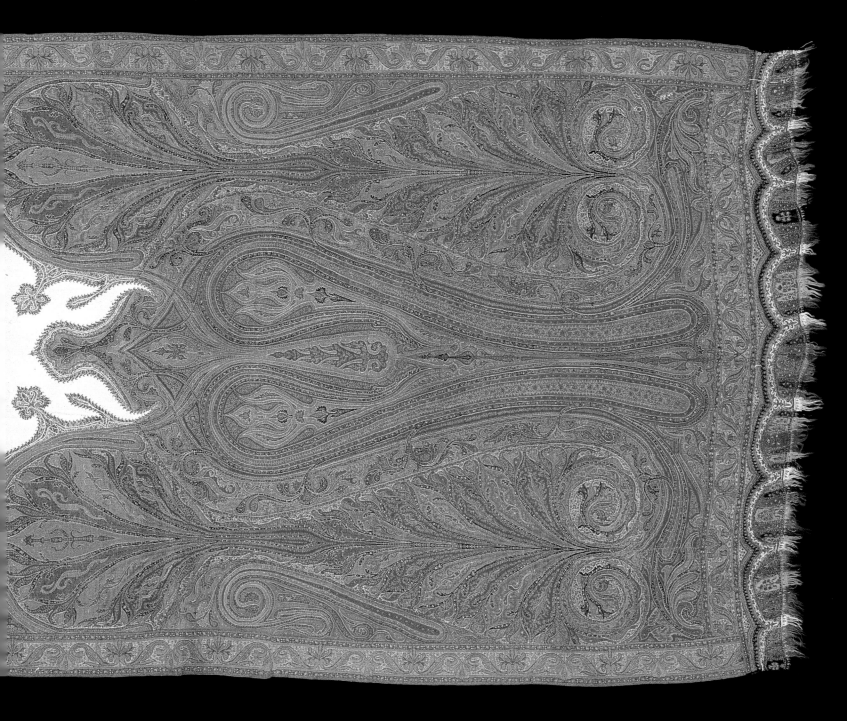

A BEAUTIFUL PINK SHAWL IS NOTICEABLE IN THE ATTIRE OF THE NOBLES, SIKH PERIOD, 19TH CENTURY.

visitor, Major General W.G. Osborne, met Ranjeet Singh in his court in 1838. He described the court: 'The floor was covered with rich shawl carpets and a gorgeous shawl canopy, embroidered with gold and precious stones and supported on golden pillars, covered three parts of the hall.' Sir Henry Fane, the British Commander-in-Chief in India, remarked on the superb dresses and jewels found even at the camp that was set up when the ruler was on the move. The camp was luxuriously furnished with tents and beds of shawl clothes. Madam Emily Eden, sister of Governor General Lord Auckland, wrote of the court: 'It reduces European magnificence to a very low pitch.'

After the Sikh rulers, Kashmir had been handed over by the British to Maharaja Gulab Singh of Jammu in 1846. During this period, embroidery became popular. Woven and embroidered shawls were made and marketed for the European and

Far-Eastern market. English and French weavers also started imitating Kashmir shawls in England and France, which has been discussed in detail by J. Irwin and M. L. Strauss.

This brief account of archaeological findings in India and outside India, ancient and medieval literary evidence, and travellers' accounts reveals that the tradition of woollen fabrics existed since the Indus Civilization. Before the fourteenth-fifteenth centuries, shawl weaving was a cottage industry around the Himalayan region that got new life during the reign of Sultan Zain-ul-Abidin in Kashmir. As for the natural production of extremely fine fabric, it came about under the able supervision of early Mughal rulers, when royal *karkhanas* were set up and Akbar took major steps for the improvement of the shawl industry. His successors and those who ruled Kashmir also contributed to the development of the industry. Today, when this splendid industry is struggling for survival, it becomes important to understand its glorious past.

A COSTUME ILLUSTRATES FINE FLORAL BUTIES, PASHMINA, KASHMIR, 19TH CENTURY.

MATERIALS AND METHODS:
MAKING THE SHAWL

Soft, attractive, and elegant Kashmiri shawls are the result of the weavers' skills in colouring, designing, embellishing and the use of fine fabrics. The geographical position of the Kashmir valley, the northwest region of India, is also vital in providing the finest and softest fleece, the main source of wool. After cleaning and processing, the fleece is used for creating woollen items.

The principle source for wool was a Central Asian species of the mountain goat. Although goats were the main source of shawl wool, a similar fleece was obtained from wild Himalayan mountain sheep such as the Shapo *(Ovis orientalis vignei)*, Argali *(Ovis ammon)*, Bharal *(Pseudois nayaur)* and the Himalayan ibex *(Capra ibex)*. The quality of wool usually depends on the climate and the altitude at which the animal is found. The shawl goat, which lives on a higher altitude and a colder climate, has the finer fleece and the thicker coat. The natural habitat of such wool-producing species is on very high altitudes, nearly above 4,500 metres (14,750 ft).

FACING PAGE: A CALICO PRINT WITH ONE BASIC DESIGN THAT HAS BEEN MODIFIED AND USED IN PASHMINA AND OTHER COSTUMES.

Wool-producing animals found at lower elevations in the Himalayan Mountains are called *khar-tehr*. These animals are almost similar to the other species, but do not possess a fine coat or long horns. The oldest male species are found close to the snowline in August-September, and the females are often seen above the forest limit. As the snow falls, the animals descend towards the valleys, but never leave the precipices except to graze on adjacent grassy slopes.

Wool from Tibet is called *chokul*. Largely, wool is derived from two kinds of sources—the domesticated shawl goat, *Capra hircus*, and from a variety of non-domesticated animals. Wool obtained from the domestic shawl goat is called pashm, widely used by Kashmiris for making the pashmina fabric. Wool from the non-domesticated or wild species is called *asli tus*, and can be obtained from three sources: the wild shawl goat, the Tibetan ibex and the Tibetan antelope. Moorcroft mentions the *baral*, which has a beautiful brown under-fleece, and resembles both the deer and the sheep. In this context, the deer's identification with the *ranku*, as mentioned in Sanskrit literature, is interesting. The *ranku* deer could perhaps be the Himalayan ibex, as

WOMAN AT WORK SPINNING WOOL FOR SHAWL, SKETCH OF J.L. KIPLING, AMRITSAR, 1870.

A MAN MAKES A SHUTTLE FROM WOOD FOR WEAVING SHAWL, SKETCH OF J.L. KIPLING, AMRITSAR, 1870.

identified in later-period texts, such as the *Maskari*. Alexander Cunningham refers to a species of wild goat of which the male was called *Rapho-chhe* and the female *Ramo-chhe*.

Generally, all wool-producing species found on very high altitudes have two layers of fleece growth, outer and inner. The outer coat is comparatively brittle, while the inner growth of fleece functions as a protective layer against the icy winds. Wool derived from the portion lying between the under-neck and the underbelly is of the finest quality. However, the hair of the outer coat plays no part in the fabrication of *kani* pashmina; it is diverted to some other use.

All kinds of raw materials or natural wools were obtained from the northwest Himalayan region of India and Tibet. Earlier, the best wool came form Changthang (the southern mountainous regions of Khotan), and Rudok (the former constituency of Ladakh). Spiti was also a wool-producing centre, but the quality of wool was of a lower grade, referred to as *Lena* in Tibetan. In 1783, the English ambassador to Tibet, Turner, visited the area and wrote in his memoirs that the Central Asian mountain goat was 'probably the most beautiful of all wool-producing goats'. Prior to 1800, the most commonly used varieties, pashmina and *asli tus,* were obtained from

28

THE MATERIAL

Shah-tus, pashm, and *raffle* are the three most popular varieties of natural wool used in Kashmir for making fabrics. *Shah-tus* is made of two words, *shah* (king) and *tus* (wool), and thus means the garb of a king, and is considered to be the finest, softest, lightest, and best wool. More extensively used is pashm, a Persian term for wool. The fabrics from pashm are known as Pashmina in India, although in the West both the animal and its fleece are denoted by the term. *Raffle* appears to be a later addition and is considered inferior in quality than the other two. *Raffle* used to be machine-spun wool derived from merino sheep. When around the nineteenth century, wool was adulterated with lesser quality fibres—such as camel, dog or yak hair—to meet demand and that was what *raffle* came to be.

MEN AT WORK IN THE SHAWL LOOM, SKETCH OF J.L. KIPLING, AMRITSAR, 1870.

Ladakh and Western Tibet. Then, wool-giving animals and fleece were procured from Yarkand and Khotan. After 1800, a fresh source for procuring the pashm was goats reared in the Tienshan Mountains, the prime marts being Turfan and Ush Turfan. The Himalayan and Tibetan regions always remained the main source.

The colour of the pashm wool depends on the colour of the shawl goat's hair. If the colour was white, the pashm wool would be the white, but if it were any other colour, irrespective of the shade of the outer coat, the pashm would tend towards a shade of brown. As far as the price of *tus* is concerned, the white colour always fetches 33 to 50 per cent more than the darker hues because it is easiest to dye in any colour. In this context, the *Ain-i-Akbari's* account

regarding the natural colours of the *tus* shawl is important. It says that 'black, white, and red were the colours of *tus*'. The white and red are understandable, but the addition of black is confusing.

The special wool-producing goat of the Central Himalayan species has its own place in the special process of making the woollen fabric in Kashmir. All types of woollen fabrics produced in Kashmir are technically divided into two broad divisions, *Kanikar* and *Amlikar*. The *Kanikar* or *Kani* is the highest form of weaving.

The *kani* pashmina were woven in the double-interlock twill tapestry technique. (Here, 'double

29

interlock' refers to the two weft-ends interlocking on each row; twill tapestry refers to the manipulation of selected heddles, vertical cords with a centre loop that guides the warp threads at selected frequencies. This leads to the development of the twill weave, where the weft is turned back to form areas of colour interlocked at the edges.) The Kashmir loom has four treadles since the preferred weave is twill.

Amlikar or *Amli*, on the other hand, is embroidery work done on the woven fabric and shawl. The darning, stem, *sujani*, *sozankar*, satin, *chikandari*, *rezkar*, *watchikan*, *jalakdozi*, and chain stitches are used for embroidering.

Cleaning, dyeing, and processing

There are twelve to fourteen stages between the collection of pashm wool and the weaving of the pashmina fabric. Each step involves a specialist, giving Kashmiri fabrics their high quality. In the summer, most wool-producing species travel from higher altitudes to low heights, and the animals shed their coat by rubbing their backs on the rocks. (It has also been suspected that species were poached and killed to get their coat to meet the high demand of *tus*.) Apart from the natural shedding of inner fleece, the domesticated goat was sheared with a knife once a year at the commencement of summer. Scissors were not used because they allowed the inner and outer layers of fleece to mix. Thus, the outer hair was cut first and the under-fleece (the inner fleece) combed towards the head and cut off progressively. Even after taking such care, there was some admixture of hair and this had to be sorted out manually—a painstaking and time-consuming process.

After cutting and segregating, the wool was collected at marts where Kashmiri weavers bought the material. Different historical periods had different marts. For instance, around the eighteenth century there was a mart in the Changthang area at Rudok (Ladakh). The wool was loaded onto backs of sheep and sent to Leh, from where it was transported to Srinagar.

Once the weavers obtain the raw wool, it went through several rounds of cleaning and dyeing. First, the fleece was sorted by hand according to the quality of the wool and the length of the fibres. Generally, a hair could be as long as 41 cm (16 in) but not exceed 91 cm (36 in). Fibres of similar length were put together, the wool was washed with plain water to rid it of dust, straw, thorns, and burrs. Soap was never used for cleaning, as Moorcroft mentioned, because it makes the wool harsh and rough. Once the wool was clear of impurities, it was pulled apart to loosen and separate entangled fibres. Traditionally, this teasing is carried out with two wooden combs. A lock of wool was placed on one comb; another comb was put on top and the wool fibres drawn between the two. The un-twined wool was ready to be spun into yarn. To give extra strength to the yarn, the cleaned wool was spread on board and a paste of pounded rice and water rubbed into it. When the wool dried and had been teased out, it was spun into thread. Traditionally, women used to do this laborious part of the work. Spinning was done on a small wooden spindle called *takli*, which allowed the spinner to rotate and move around.

The yarn was ready to be woven into fabric, which was spun to make two quality threads. A higher number of twists were given to the threads, thereby strengthening the yarn, so that it could be used as a warp thread. Less twisting made the weft thread. The weft thread was not as strong as the warp thread because it did not go through the same kind of tension and friction as the warp thread. The weft thread gave the yarn a fluffy texture, helping to create beautiful motifs.

A GROUP OF CRAFTSMEN ARE BUSY EMBROIDERING, COMPANY SCHOOL, 19TH CENTURY.

The next important step was the dyeing of the yarn, which was done by the *rangrez* or dyer. Usually woollen fabrics were woven with yarns of natural shades, but to create designs various colourful dyed yarns were required. The *rangrez*'s work was vital and specialised, the occupation invariably being hereditary. During the first half of the nineteenth century, many visitors came to Kashmir and recorded the colours used by the dyers and their possible source. Before using any dye, the *rangrez* takes two things into considerations. First, the natural dyes, which were obtained from selected plants, insects, *lac*, and other material. *Lac* was obtained from the insect, *Kerria lacca*, and red and pink colours were derived from it. For blue and green dyes, the indigo plant *Indigofera tinctoria*, was the source. Two, the *rangrez* chose the whitest wool available among all the shades of white since it accepted the brilliant dye and the use of fine goat wool as compared to sheep wool. As per Moorcroft's account, during the Mughal period there were more than three hundred colours available for

31

SCIENCE AND KASHMIR DYES

Penelope Rogers and George Taylor of Textile Research Associates, US, made a detailed study of the dyestuffs of Kashmiri shawls. They studied a limited range of around twenty-seven differently coloured yarns from eight shawls that were tested by absorption spectrophotometry and thin-layer chromatography. Analysis showed a relatively limited range of dyestuffs: only five or six dyes. The Kashmiri weaver's wide palette of colours seems to have been achieved then by varying the strength of the dye and by combining one dye with another. It is interesting to note that the distribution of the colours was regulated by the thickness of the thread, the thinner threads being appropriated to the lighter tints. The study indicates the high standards of the *rangrez*. More studies will help understand the dyeing system practised by the *rangrez*.

dying shawl wool. But, at the beginning of the nineteenth century there were sixty-four tints. The falling figure indicates the declining status of dyers during the early nineteenth century.

After the yarn is prepared, it was taken to the *pennakam gurn* or warp-dresser, who dipped it into boiled rice water to stiffen each thread and set it apart from the rest. The job of the warp-dressers is to twist the threads into the required thickness, which gives warp yarns more strength and weight than the weft. Warp yarns measuring 3.5 yards and consisting of two to three thousand threads were double in number than the weft yarns. While weaving, silk yarn was also used for the warp on the border of a shawl. The use of silk conferred many advantages—such as the prominent reflection of the darker shade of the dyed wool. Since the silk is hard and has strength, it also gave more body to the edge of the cloth.

Once the warp is ready, the pattern needs to be made. Enter the *ukash* or the pattern-drawer, who started by working out the complete design, generally, in black and white with charcoal pencils. The design then went to the hands of the *tarfarash* or *gandanwol*, who decided on the proportion of differently coloured yarns to be required. Sometimes two different people did this work and sometimes the same worker. From *gandanwol*, the *talim* guru took down the particulars in a coded pattern and delivered a copy of the document to the weaver. Next the *tilis* (needles) were prepared, each *tilis* armed with differently coloured yarns. The needles made of light and smooth wood are without eyes (probably that is why the technique is known as *kani*) and both their sharp ends are slightly charred to prevent their becoming rough or jagged through working. Under the superintendence of the *gandanwol*, the weavers knotted the yarn of the *tilis* to the warp. The face or the right side of the cloth was placed next to the ground. The work of weaving was carried on from the back or reverse side of the fabric on which the needles *(tilis)* were disposed in a row. The number of *tilis* could vary from 400 to 1,500 according to the lightness or the pattern chosen for the fabric.

The technique used in weaving Kashmir shawls is twill tapestry. In the process, the weft does not pass from selvedge to selvedge as in tapestry but is turned back to form areas of colour interlinked at the edges. Working on the reverse side of the fabric, the weavers interlocked the coloured weft threads, producing a slight ridge where the joints were made. They were raised and two-coloured on the back, but invisible on the right side. This twill-tapestry technique resulted in the border being stronger than the single-colour field whose fragile, almost transparent material does not wear well and has to be completely replaced when damaged. Twill tapestry is a slow process, but it can produce any design.

Apart from *kani* weaving the other important variety of Kashmir shawls are the *amli* or embroidered shawls. Entire pashmina and *tus* shawls were embroidered with pashm*a*, silk or *zari* threads and became popular in the beginning of the nineteenth century.

The entire pattern is woven with coloured *tilis*. The finished shawls or fabrics are then submitted to the *purzagur* or cleaner, who sorts out the knots of the discoloured hair or yarn. He either pulls these threads out severally with a pair of tweezers or shaves out the defects. The fabric is then sent directly to the *rafugar,* who does the mending and gives final shape to the shawl or fabric. As the complete shawl or fabric passes through many hands, it becomes dirty. So, before it goes for sale, it is given a final wash which also helps remove the stiffness due to the rice starch in the thread. After washing, the shawl is dried in the shade, as the hot sun spoils the colours. Finally, the shawl becomes fine and soft and ready for sale.

This process was adopted by Kashmiri weavers, according to accounts of several travellers, for selecting the raw material, cleaning, spinning, dyeing, weaving and embroidery.

DESIGNS ON THE LOOM:
THE KANIKAR STYLE

'At the end of the sixteenth century, when the *Ain-i-Akbari* was compiled, a *paramnaram* shawl cost from 2 rupiya to 20 murh. By 1823 the manufacturer's price (according to Moorcroft's document housed at India Office Library, London - MSS.Eur. D. 264) for a plain shawl with a narrow edging of coloured yarn was fifty to sixty rupees, but for a piece having an ornamented band running all round the shawl between the border and the field the price was from Rs 100 to Rs 2,300 a pair.'

Today, the price of Kashmiri shawls is in the thousands depending upon the material, workmanship, and design. Shawls woven with intricate patterns have always attracted a good price. One main way of drawing a pattern on the shawl was via weaving or *kanikar*, the shawl being known as a *kani* shawl. The *kani* shawls are those in which designs are created on the loom by transfixing warps and wefts and sometimes with extra wefts. The *kani* shawls are also an important factor in studies that look at, of course, the technical advancement of the loom, of the expertise of dyers in working on pashm staple yarns, of the creative skill of the design-makers and of the

weaver's knowledge. Research scholars have studied *kani* shawls to arrive at a probable date for their manufacture. John Irwin (1955 and 1972) made the first annalistic study of Kashmir shawls. He classified the *boteh* by giving an approximate period to the development of the *boteh* design. Frank Ames (1980) adopted an almost similar outline. He looked at the *boteh* pattern through the four political phases of the Kashmir valley—the Mughal, Afghan, Sikh, and Dogra—and the technical, economical, and social environment. In her study, Monique Levi-Strauss (1987) observed the European influence on Kashmiri shawls. Recently, Rogers and George Taylor of the US Textile Research Association undertook a detailed scientific study of the dyestuffs used in Kashmir shawls and found only a limited number. This contradicted several travellers' accounts that said Kashmir dyers were experts in dyeing in sixty-four shades or even three hundred colours. But this scientific study was done in a very small scale and the large-scale study would obtain a much clearer view. All these studies emphasize that it is always appropriate to study the evolution of the *boteh* pattern within the historical period, the economic and trade policies, and the social trends with due scientific rigour. A study of the shawl and other woollen pieces

FACING PAGE: DETAIL OF *CHOGA*, KASHMIR, LATE 19TH CENTURY, PASHMINA.

created between the seventeenth and nineteenth centuries basically involves a careful examination of shawls, their component parts, the slow and subtle evolution of motifs, the use of colours, raw materials and thread counts. These help lead to the date of manufacture.

Apart from the regular sized *kani* shawls, moon shawls, which were square shawls with a central circular medallion and half-corner medallions; *patka* or sash; and *jamawar* or dress material for making different costumes like the *choga* (loose outer gown used by men), *jama* (tied fitting dress), coat, jacket, *paijama* (loose trousers), *jajam* (a long rectangular spread), *rumal* (square cloth of various uses), table covers, and turbans were also made.

THE PATKA OR SASH

The *Patka*, sash or waistband, is a lengthy drape generally used by men and worn around the waist over the *choga* or *jama*. These rectangular *patkas*, which were the significant part of the costume, were wrapped two or three times around the waist with a portion of the decorated end panel hanging gracefully in the front. Attractively woven or embroidered *patkas* became popular during the Mughal period though these were considered an essential part of the dress right from the early period. Ancient literature informs us that the *patka* was known as *patti* (a Sanskrit term), *kamarpatta* or *kamarband*. According to *Cullavaga*, the Buddhist text, both men and women used to wear the *patka* during the sixth century B.C. Apart from various literary references, numerous visual references were also available in the sculptures. Portrayal of *patka* over the dhoti could be noticed on the early stone images of *yakshas,* men and women. This tradition continues and could be noticed in stone, bronze, and terracotta sculptures and coins and miniature paintings of different periods. During the Mughal period, these

1 *Field (matan)*

2 *Vertical hashia*

3 *Horizontal hashia*

4 *Pallu / End panel*

5 *End panel motif*

6 *Fringes*

The designer's patka

PATKA, MID-18TH CENTURY, PASHMINA, LOOM WOVEN, COLOUR: OFF-WHITE (B.G.); BLUE, YELLOW, BROWN, GREY, MAROON (P)
SIZE: 24 CM (H.E.P); 19.2 CM (B); 1.8 x 3 CM (H); 230 x 70 CM (F)

This off-white *patka* made from quality *pashmina* beautifully illustrates flower cluster *botehs* on the end panel within a narrow *hashia* frame. It is an attractive and special one from the design point of view. Symmetrically arranged these flower cluster *botehs* illustrate the rising centre branch of the *boteh* around which small flowers and leaves are arranged so that it all takes the shape of a cluster of *botehs*. To make it symmetric, the artist has designed leafy branches and placed the *boteh* on a small mound. This natural arrangement supports the inner movement of the flower clusters that form the cone *boteh*. Shades of yellow on the off-white background make it attractive and rare. Since these *patkas* were worn around the waist and both the end panels have to be left free, most of the early *patkas* have a plain field and a heavy end panel.

36

patkas became such an integral part of the attire that they signified the rank and status of the courtiers. Specially designed and crafted, such *patkas* were often awarded to courtiers by the emperors. The courtiers were supposed to wear the *patkas* as a part of their court costumes.

Apart from being a wrap around the costume, sometimes these *patkas* provided space for keeping small things such as thumb rings, daggers, and pen cases between layers of warp. A painting, *'Shahjahan as a prince holding a jewel,'* from the Minto album housed in the Victoria and Albert Museum, London, is a good example. This painting illustrates Prince Shahjahan wearing a beautiful *patka* over an outfit and using it to hold an archer's ring, a dagger and other items. Such a significant part of the costume was made of cotton, silk and wool at different weaving centres. Such works were beautifully ornamented with *zari* brocades, *kani* weave, block printed or painted and embroidered on silk, wool, and cotton respectively. Also, scholars have paid more attention to silk brocade *patkas* than any other material. *Patkas* were produced in the Mughal *karkhanas* and are presently housed in various museums. Some work has also been done on cotton-printed and embroidered *patkas*. Not much work has been done exclusively on the woollen *patkas* of Kashmir, although few *patkas* have been discussed by John Irwin and Frank Ames in their work on Kashmiri shawls.

As far as Mughal woollen *patkas* are concerned not many have become known so far except a few which are housed in the museums of Varanasi, Ahmedabad, Washington, D.C., Boston, London and New Delhi. These *patkas* are invariably made of *tus* or soft pashmina and off-white is the predominant colour for the *matan* or field. The length and width of these *patkas* varies; the usual length is around 155 to 480 cm while the width is between 47 and 52 cm.

According to Moorcroft, 'girdles ... for the waist or *shamlas* are eight *gaz* in length and one and a half *gaz* broad [a standard *gaz* or *ilahi* was 33 inches]'. Most *patkas* have a plain *matan* or field, though Mughal *patkas* did have an entire decorated field as in an important piece housed in the Textile Museum, Washington. Another example is in the National Museum of New Delhi. The ornamental end panels of the *patkas* illustrate *botehs*: a mélange of flowers, bent tip strawberry, pin-wheel, and flower clusters. However, the chevron pattern and rows of small flower *buties* are also represented in early Mughal *patka* or waistbands. The base of the *boteh* shows a variety of motifs. In some early *patkas*, the base of the *boteh* illustrates a small mound or vase; occasionally these vases are placed on a flat dish—a later development. Sometimes the *boteh* has a 'root-type decoration' base, the inspiration for which, scholars opine, comes from Chinese ideograms. Fine line work, colours, and good overall compositions mark these *botehs*, which were arranged symmetrically at equal distances. Most *patkas* had twisted fringes which give the attire an elegant look.

Another important aspect of the *patkas* was the horizontal and vertical *hashia*, which generally varied in size and design. Sometimes the background of the *hashia* was different from the colour of the *matan*. In most cases, the vertical *hashia* was slightly bigger than the horizontal *hashia*, which worked as a frame to the end panels. Although both the *hashias* represented a floral creeper motif, the design sometimes varied. A common motif is the floral creeper in a meandering vine formation. Occasionally a tiny flower *buti* was taken from the main *boteh* itself as is the case with the *patka* from the National Museum collection. The Bharat Kala Bhavan's *patka* illustrates an interesting example, depicting a row of disconnected sprigs rather than a meandering vine.

Woollen *patkas* mainly belong to the Mughal and Afghan phases of the shawl industry of the seventeenth and eighteenth centuries. They have all the shades and colours whether off-white, maroon red, blue, black, pink or yellow with a tint of green. Superbly designed employing these *patkas* were decorated with nice patterns, cone *boteh*, a row of tiny *buties*, flower bouquet arrangement etc. All these salient features make this collection an important one, which clearly reflects the fine fabric, artistically designed pattern and good colour combination.

Early woollen patka

PATKA, EARLY 17TH CENTURY, MUGHAL, KASHMIR, PASHMINA, LOOM WOVEN
COLOUR: MAROON (B.G.); BLUE, YELLOW, GREY, OFF-WHITE (P)
SIZE: 25 CM (H.E.P.); 19 CM (B); 4.5 x 2.5 CM (H); 576 x 68.5 CM (F)

One of the significant features of the early woollen *patkas* is the depiction of six *botehs* within the *hashia* frame on both the end panels, narrow horizontal and vertical *hashias* and a plain *matan* or centrefield. This brilliant maroon background *patka* has all these features; the most striking characteristic being its floral *boteh* at the end panel. The colourful and attractive small flowers of the *botehs* are like a rose abstraction, which resembles bent-tip strawberries. The natural downward bend of the *boteh* composed of strawberries, buds, and leaves gives the impression of the breeze. The branches on either side of the lower portion of the *boteh* give it a more balanced pattern. The domination of blue and the use of a bit of grey with a yellow outline make the colour scheme attractive and closer to the Mughal style. The narrow horizontal *hashia* depicts the typical Mughal style floral creeper that has a small flower. The slightly wider vertical *hashia* illustrates the blossoming rose creeper on a white background.

The bouquet patka

17TH CENTURY, MUGHAL, KASHMIR, PASHMINA, LOOM WOVEN

COLOUR: OFF-WHITE (B.G.); MAROON, GREY, YELLOW (P)

SIZE: 24.5 CM (H.E.P); 20 CM (B); 3 X 2 CM (H); 246 X 70 CM (F)

This superbly patterned *patka* is an exclusive example of *boteh* on both the end panels, which contain a mélange of flowers. It is also yet another impressive sample of Mughal craftsmanship. Here the artist has succeeded in achieving a balanced *boteh* that too in a bouquet form, while the field remains plain. Rich colourful blossoming roses, irises, cogwheel flowers, buds and stylised wavy leaves make it a special flower bouquet. The shading done on flowers and leaves and even on the mound from where the *boteh* starts is a significant feature of this *patka*. Maroon and shades of pink are prominent, while yellow, grey, and blue provide contrast. A narrow horizontal *hashia* depicts a similar floral creeper, while a vertical *hashia* illustrates the angular floral *buties* in creeper design. Interestingly, the blue leaf creeper is on both the *hashias*.

Patka with cone botehs

PATKA, c.1800 CENTURY, KASHMIR,
PASHMINA, LOOM WOVEN
COLOUR: PINKISH (B.G.); MAROON,
BLUE, GREEN, YELLOW, GREY, WHITE (P)
SIZE: 30.5 CM (H.E.P.); 24.5 CM (B);
3.5 x 2.5 CM (H); 648 x 70 CM (F)

Around early 1800, a significant change in the composition of the *boteh* was noticed on the end panels of the Kashmir shawls, the row of single flower *buties* was replaced by a row of cone *botehs* and the number of *botehs* was decreased. This pinkish plain *matan patka* is a good example of that change. It is decorated with a colourful row of six elongated cone *botehs*. The maroon, blue, yellow, and white elongated cone *botehs* provide a good contrast to the pink background, which illustrates a cluster of flowers, tiny flowers, leaves, and a full-blown flower on the top with small projections. These *botehs* start from the vase that rests on a dish. A full-blown flower on top of the *boteh* makes it impressive. Both the *hashia* illustrate the meandering vine design on an off-white background and fringes add grace to it.

41

18th-century's favourite patka

PATKA, 18TH CENTURY, KASHMIR, PASHMINA, LOOM WOVEN
COLOUR: YELLOWISH GREEN (B.G.); MAROON, BLUE, GREY, WHITE (P)
SIZE: 26.5 CM (H.E.P.); 23 CM (B.S.); 3 x 2.2 CM (H); 480 x 65.5 CM (F)

This brilliant yellowish green Kashmiri shawl was very popular during the eighteenth century as many Sikh and Pahari school miniature paintings illustrate such shawls; the shawls were worn by important personalities. Yellow with a tinge of green makes this *patka* an important example. It has six elongated cone *botehs* on the end panel and a meandering vine *hashia*. The elongated cone is composed of different types of small flowers, leaves, and creepers emerging from the vase. The vase itself is placed on a raised mound for a balanced composition. The saw tooth leaf comes out from the vase and descends, making the *patka* very beautiful.

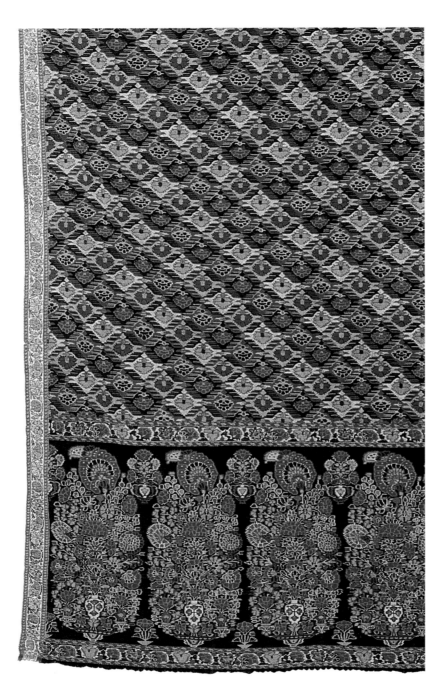

Afghan-period patka

PATKA, C.1800 CENTURY, KASHMIR,
PASHMINA, LOOM WOVEN
COLOUR: BLACK (B.G.); MAROON, PINK,
GREY, LIGHT YELLOW, WHITE, GREEN (P)
SIZE: 32 CM (H.E.P); 26 CM (B);
3 X 2.5 CM (H); 480 X 83.5 CM (F)

The black *patka* is an extraordinary example of Afghan-period *patkas*, which have a chequered-design *matan* and elongated cone *botehs* on both the end panels. Although these cone *botehs* are done in a manner similar to earlier *patka* pieces, the treatment of the *boteh* is more elaborate and stereotyped, losing the natural look. The cone *boteh* that emerges from a vase is placed on a flat dish, but the number of vases has increased: instead of a single vase, two small vases are depicted on either side of the bigger vase. Between each pair of *botehs* at the base and the top is a small single-flower *boteh* that fills the field with the flower pattern. The entire field of the *patka* is decorated in a chequered design that represents the blossoming flower motif in a contrasting background. Both *hashias* depict a creeper with different flowers. The horizontal *hashia* is worked with silk thread.

Striped patka

Striped patka, c.1810-30, Kashmir,
Pashmina, loom woven
Colour: Off-white, maroon, black
(b.g.); yellow, light blue, green,
pink, blue (p)
Size: 40 cm (h.e.p); 35 cm (b);
2.5 cm (h = horizontal);
480 x 74 cm (f)

This elegantly woven *patka* is beautifully ornamented with stripes all over the field, an elongated *coif boteh* on the end panels, and a *hashia* that is a good example of Afghan-period Kashmir craftsmanship. Maroon and off-white stripes alternate over the entire *matan*, which illustrates tiny, multi-coloured *buties*. The end panel of the *patka* depicts six large, closely woven *kalka* or mosaic *coif botehs*, which have a chromatic and colourful arrangement of flowers with a rose on the top. Between each pair of *botehs* at the base are small *botehs* and an additional flower branch or garland bent towards the cone's tip. The *boteh's* chromatic scheme is distinguished by a profusion of maroon, pink or yellow flowers on a black ground. A vase with a round base and a narrow mouth is placed on the mound that has an illustration with a radial arrangement. The triangular mound is placed on a dish.

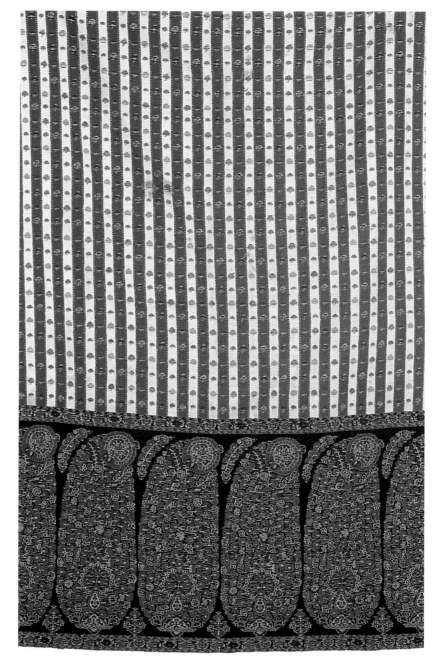

Tiny buti patka

PATKA, 19TH CENTURY, KASHMIR, PASHMINA, LOOM
WOVEN
COLOUR: BLUE (B.G.); MAROON, PINK, GREEN, WHITE (P)
SIZE: 19.5 CM (H.E.P); 1.2 CM (B); 3 x 2.5 CM (H);
328 x 70 CM (F)

The plain deep blue *matan* of this *patka* has beautifully decorated end panels and *hashias*. The end panels illustrate tiny *buties,* which are symmetrically arranged in rows, reminiscent of the early fashion of Mughal-style *buti* compositions. A similar kind of *buti* arrangement done on a shawl is in the Victoria and Albert museum, London. The end panel of such *patkas* is not very broad as compared to elongated *botehs* depicted in the end panels. Both the *hashias* have a green background and depict small, pink-green *buties* which provide a good colour combination and make it more attractive.

The chequered patka

FACING PAGE

PATKA, 19TH CENTURY, KASHMIR, PASHMINA, LOOM WOVEN
COLOUR: MAROONISH RED (B.G.); BLUE, YELLOW, GREEN, WHITE, PINK (P)
SIZE: 36 CM (H.E.P); 31 CM (B); 2.5 CM (H);110 x 48 CM (F)

This long *patka* has a chequered field, colourful end panels, and a *hashia*. The end panel depicts three big *coif botehs* (appearing to be incomplete in width). The entire field of the *patka* is worked in a chequered pattern using a saw-tooth leave pattern and each chequered unit is decorated with a pattern of tiny flowers. These end panel *botehs* are mainly composed of a mélange of flowers around a central, symmetrical plant growing from a vase in a flat inverted dish with a raised foot and a radial top rose. One small vase having a radial flower arrangement is placed on either side of the big vase. Stylised, drooping leaves are also placed near the smaller vases. Between each pair of *botehs* at the base is a small single flower *buta* surrounded by flowers and placed on a small mound. An additional flower branch or garland is bent towards the tip of the *boteh*.

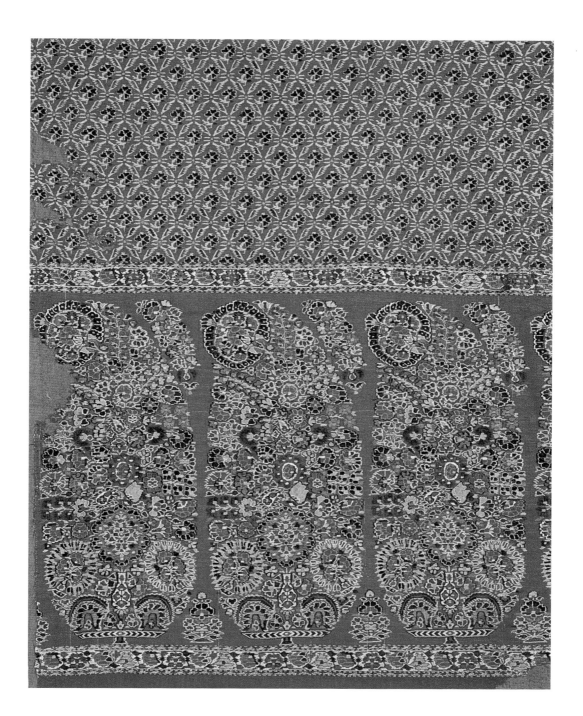

47

The long patka

PATKA, MID-19TH CENTURY, KASHMIR,
PASHMINA, LOOM WOVEN
COLOUR: MAROONISH RED (B); GREEN,
YELLOW, WHITE, BLUE, PINK, MAROON
SIZE: 44 CM (H.E.P); 43.5 CM (B);
9.5 CM (H); 320 X 50 CM (F)

The last in this group is the long *patka* with a narrow width, beautiful field decoration and elaborate *boteh* pattern at the end panels. The rich, red field of the *patka* illustrates the *kalka buties* and the leaf pattern between the *buties*. The end panel depicts two elaborate *kalka botehs*, a curved, pointed tip on either side. The *boteh* depicts a big vase having a radial flower at its lower portion, which illustrates the small *kalka buties* and leaves. Between the *kalka botehs*, a long *chinar* leaf pattern is woven. It is elaborately decorated with stylised flowers and curved leaves on a white background. The horizontal *hashia* depicts the floral creeper in a colourful manner; the vertical *hashia* has only a green piping.

The plain, striped and chequered design fields of these *patkas* are beautifully decorated with attractive designs on the end panel. They add grace to the costume, which makes it a vital part of the attire. This can be visually seen in a number of miniature paintings of the Mughal, Deccani, Rajasthani and Pahari schools.

THE MOON SHAWL

The square shawls of Kashmir are known as *Chaukora* (the Hindi term for a cloth with four equal corners) and *Chandar* or as the moon shawls. Generally, these are square; sometimes rectangular or longish moon shawls were also made as per the requirement of the patron or the market. Usually, moon shawls have a plain centre field with a circular medallion in the centre and a quarter medallion in all the four corners. Some of the moon shawls were beautifully decorated with the patterns on the centre field, while the composition of all the five medallions remains the same. Generally, moon shawls are surrounded with a *hashia* all round the edges like any other shawl while fringes at two ends add beauty. The colour schemes, designs and patterns of such moon shawls are attractive and balanced, which gives them a special place in the entire Kashmiri shawl collection.

In the middle of the eighteenth century, when Kashmir came under the direct control of the Afghans (1753 – 1819) such moon shawls were probably introduced in near Eastern markets and soon became popular in Turkey and Iran. By the nineteenth century, moon shawls became popular in the European market also. Folded diagonally, these shawls were used as a drape over the shoulder—a style that can be noticed in a number of miniature and oil paintings of the eighteenth-nineteenth centuries. Occasionally, these shawls were used as a head covering around the turbans, still the practice in some Arab countries. Apart from the draping style, these shawls became popular because they were smaller than traditional shawls, took less time to weave and cost less.

As far as the antiquity of the moon shawls is concerned, no such shawls belonging to the Mughal period are known. However, there are several exceptionally beautiful moon shawls from the Afghan period housed in various Indian museums and abroad. In general, early moon shawls are comparatively smaller in size, have a plain field, even the size of the circular centre and half-corner medallions is small, and there is a narrow *hashia* all around the shawl. From the later Afghan period, these moon shawls depict repeated *buties* (sprigs of small flowers) on the centre field. Apart from this simple *buti* pattern, some moon shawls were decorated with a striking arrangement of checkerboards which depict patterns made of small ducks or had a zigzag form.

During the Sikh period (1819 – 1846), shawls became more popular and changes were observed in design, colour, pattern and technique. This change appeared on the moon shawls. The foremost change occurred with the size of the moon shawl: it changed from 130 x 130 cm to 160 x 160 cm. The new-sized moon shawl was decorated with brighter colours and heavily patterned. Most Sikh period moon shawls were intricately woven with various designs such as *kalka*, pine *buta* or *buti*, crescent and hooked vine. Another prominent Sikh style, which continued during the Dogra period (1846–1877), was to prepare the moon shawl in parts. Separate *kani* pieces were woven independently and later joined together to form a moon shawl. The narrow *hashia* of the early moon shawls developed into the broad *hashia*. In the later-phase moon shawl, the horizontal and vertical *hashias* were worked differently. The horizontal *hashia* was woven with the shawl illustrating a pattern similar to the centre field. The vertical *hashias*, which were in stripes, were either woven separately and stitched on later or occasionally plain piping was attached to the edges. The conventional moon shawls of the Sikh period have multicoloured stripes of plain pashmina cloth as fringes. Such outermost edge decorations were added only to two horizontal ends of the shawls.

The last variety, moon shawls of the Dogra period, were composed of many pieces, and it is not difficult to find such shawls containing literally hundreds of pieces. These patchwork shawls were made in great quantity after 1850. Moon shawls were made from many small pashmina stripes, each measuring about 8 cm in length, and embroidered with the *mehrab* (arch shaped) motif. During this period, the colour scheme became brighter, the contrasts were vibrant, and the European influence on the designs could be seen. The moon shawl collection in the National Museum is vivid and colourful. Most shawls belong to the Afghan, Sikh, and Dogra periods and have a variety of designs and dimensions. Such good examples clearly reflect that a bigger market existed for the moon shawl around the eighteenth-nineteenth century.

Guide:
b = background; c. med. = central medallion; f = full; h = *hashia*; p = pattern

Khartreez moon shawl

MID-18TH CENTURY, PASHMINA, LOOM WOVEN
COLOUR: OFF-WHITE, PEACH STRIPES (B); YELLOW, BLUE & MAROON (P)
SIZE: 27 x 28 CM (C. MED.); 3 x 3 CM (H); 123 x 130 CM (F)

An exceptionally beautiful variety of moon shawls is the *khatreez* type, which is a good example of perfect colour balance and shade. Moreover, an unusual depiction of *kalka* or *kalgha* motif on the quarter medallions makes it rare. The most interesting part of this moon shawl is the weaving technique used for the medallions, which gives the impression that medallions have been placed on the *khatreez* background. Off-white and peach coloured alternate stripes are in the background and each stripe is artistically decorated with tiny floral *buties*. The most fascinating feature of this moon shawl is the corner medallion, which is different from the central medallion. All medallions are embellished with tiny floral motifs and prominently with a blue four-petal floral pattern in the central medallion and a *kalka* or *kalgha* motif in the corner medallions. This might be one of the early depictions of *kalka* pattern in weaving. The floral pattern of the *hashia* and the twisted fringes are the special attractions of this moon shawl.

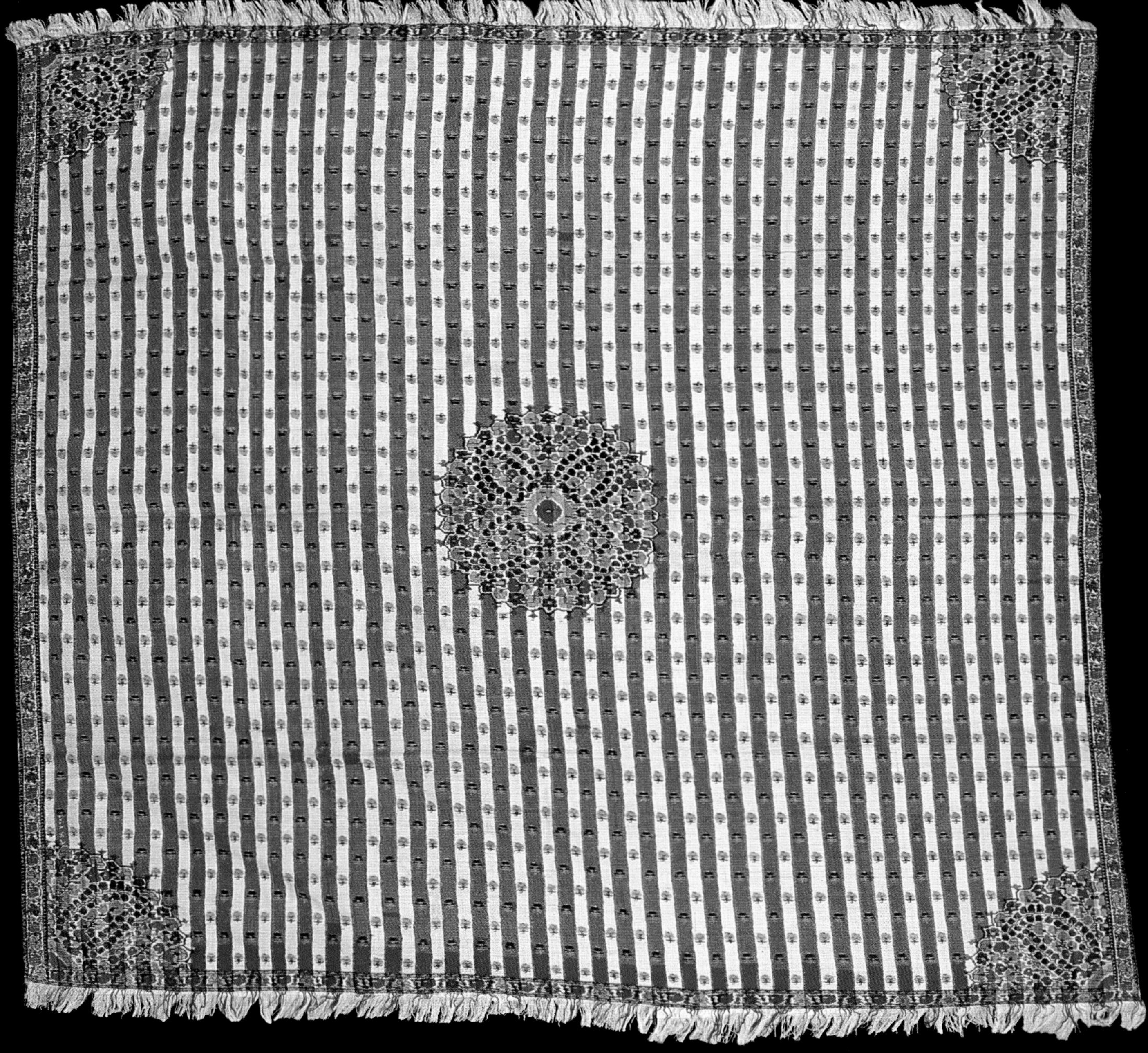

Classic moon shawl

MOON SHAWL, MID-18TH CENTURY, KASHMIR, PASHMINA, LOOM WOVEN
COLOUR: OFF-WHITE (B); BLUE, MAROON & GREY (P)
SIZE: 28.5 x 23 CM (C. MED.); 2.5 x 2 CM (H); 130 x 122 CM (F)

This fine pashmina moon shawl is an early example. It shows the circular blue medallion in the centre, quarter medallions at the corners, and a narrow *hashia* running all along the four sides illustrating the meandering vine pattern. Combination of blue with maroon on an off-white background makes this moon shawl attractive. The medallions are intricately woven with small floral *buties*, further surmounted by a maroon outline done in the zigzag pattern. Although maroon is used sparingly, it helps break the monotony and gives a natural look reminiscent of Mughal-style decoration. There are skilfully twisted fringes on two sides.

The colourful shawl

MOON SHAWL, LAST QUARTER OF
18TH CENTURY, PASHMINA, LOOM
WOVEN
COLOUR: OFF-WHITE (B); YELLOW,
MAROON, BLUE & BLACK (P)
SIZE: 25.5 x 25.5 CM (C. MED.);
2.8 x 2.8 CM (H);
130 x 126 CM (F)

This almost square moon shawl is fully decorated with small, winged-shape polychrome *buties* in maroon, yellow, blue and black. The small central medallion beautifully illustrates the floral pattern and quarter corner medallions depict a flower motif. The zigzag outline in blue is on the outer edge of the medallions, which appear like a star. This makes the shawl more colourful and artistic. The narrow *hashia* with the bent-tip strawberry, full blossom rose and pointed leaf flower alternately runs all around the moon shawl.

53

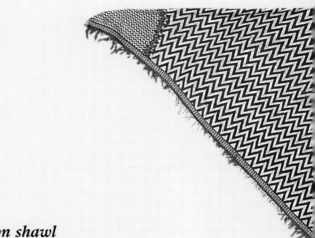

Zigzag moon shawl

Early 18th century, pashmina, loom woven
Colour: off-white and green (all over);
maroon, blue, yellow, and white (p)
Size: 42 x 41 cm (c. med.); 2.5 x 2 cm (h);
114 x 130 cm (f)

The popular Persian chevron or zigzag pattern, which symbolises flowing water, is reminiscent of the Persian influence on the Mughal style, which can be seen in architecture, in textile, and even in woollen shawls. Green and the off-white zigzag pattern is beautifully illustrated in this moon shawl, probably created especially for the Far Eastern market. By using diverse directions and differently sized zigzag patterns, the artist has succeeded in creating variations. The field illustrates the bigger size of the chevron while the centre and quarter medallions have smaller zigzag patterns. The outer edges of the medallions are decorated with a narrow creeper band in maroon and blue. Both the *hashias* are worked in a zigzag pattern in maroon and off-white in the horizontal direction. The twisted fringes on the horizontal side suggest that this side was well used for draping.

FOLLOWING PAGES 56-57

Bordered moon shawl

LAST QUARTER OF 18TH CENTURY, KASHMIR, PASHMINA, LOOM WOVEN
COLOUR: MAROON (B); BLUE, GREEN, YELLOW, WHITE, PINK & BLACK (P)
SIZE: 48 x 43.5 CM (C. MED.); 3 x 1.5 CM (H); 143 x 140 CM (F)

Superbly designed, this moon shawl depicts ogee arches on the entire field and has two broad end panels on the horizontal side—the most significant feature. Around the last quarter of the eighteenth century, the ogee pattern, often used in Turkish and Persian architecture, was noticed in shawls and *jamawar*. The entire field of this moon shawl portrays the ogee pattern in yellow, green, and white and a four-petal, small flower motif is in between each ogee arch. Centre and quarter medallions also follow a similar pattern. Nine bigger size *kalka botehs* are on either side of the horizontal end panel and are arranged in compartments divided by the leaf pattern. The narrow *hashia* illustrating the meandering vine pattern lends beauty to this moon shawl. The bordered moon shawl appears to be made on order.

55

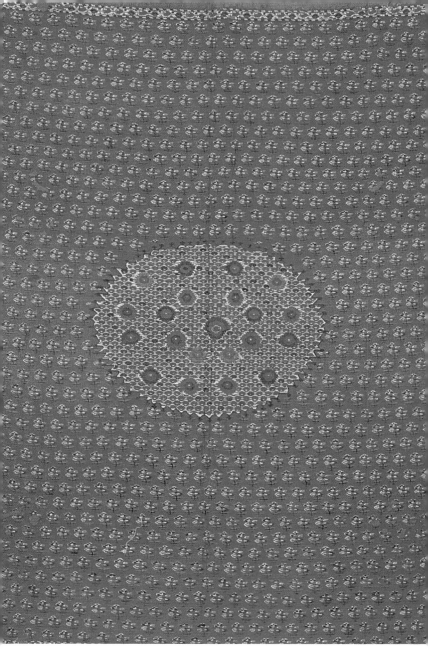

LAST QUARTER OF 18TH CENTURY, KASHMIR, PASHMINA, LOOM WOVEN

COLOUR: MAROON (B); BLUE, GREEN, YELLOW & WHITE (P)

SIZE: 43.5 x 55.5 CM (C. MED.); 3 x 2 CM (H); 171 x 160 CM (F)

Moon shawls began with the plain field and were then decorated with the zigzag and ogee patterns or sometimes with end panels. They are the few important eighteenth-century pieces. In the nineteenth century, a few changes in the size, the colourful background and design occurred in the moon shawls. This late eighteenth century, rectangular moon shawl has different features as compared to earlier ones. It has three-flower *buties* all over the field. The bigger circular central and quarter size corner medallions are worked in a mosaic-style floral arrangement on a red background. Vertical and horizontal *hashias* depict different floral motifs. The vertical *hashia* illustrates the bent-tip strawberry rose flower while the horizontal *hashia* portrays the floral creeper.

FOLLOWING PAGE 60

Sikh period shawl

EARLY 19TH CENTURY, KASHMIR, PASHMINA, LOOM WOVEN

COLOUR: OFF-WHITE (B); MAROON, BLUE, GREEN (P)

SIZE: 69 x 56 CM (C. MED.); 8.2 CM (VERTICAL H);

164 x 144 CM (F)

The elaborate design and the use of many bright colours are the salient features of the Sikh period moon shawl. This off-white shawl illustrates a serrated group of three *kalka botehs*, one big and two small, symmetrically arranged all over. These *kalka botehs* have been woven between the oblong circle and the arching U-shape motifs that make it an interesting pattern. The rest of the field is worked with a hooked vine and leaf motif. The central and corner medallions are woven in a typical mosaic pattern of the nineteenth century. The broad horizontal *hashia* of the moon shawl depicts stylised floral creepers, while the vertical *hashia* is plain. Silk lining and *zari* piping are all around the shawl—perhaps a later addition that gives the impression that it had a rich owner.

FOLLOWING PAGE 61

The two-piece style

MID-19TH CENTURY, AMRITSAR / KASHMIR,

PASHMINA, LOOM WOVEN

COLOUR: OFF-WHITE (B); MAROON, BLUE,

GREEN & YELLOW (P)

SIZE: 61 x 61 CM (C. MED.); 9 CM (VERTICAL H);

195 x 178 CM (F)

The last moon shawl of this lot is rectangular and made of more than two pieces stitched together lengthwise. Center and corner medallions are in the ogee pattern in maroon. A full flower motif is arranged at each intersection of the pattern. The entire field is decorated with *kalka*, leaf, and bud designs. Broad horizontal *hashia* depict a wheel-shaped motif and squarish floral design alternately. The other edges of the moon shawl are without a *hashia*.

Moon shawls were especially made for a particular market and they did not last, as long shawls became more popular by the end of the twentieth century. But these shawls had sufficient variations to make this group an interesting collection.

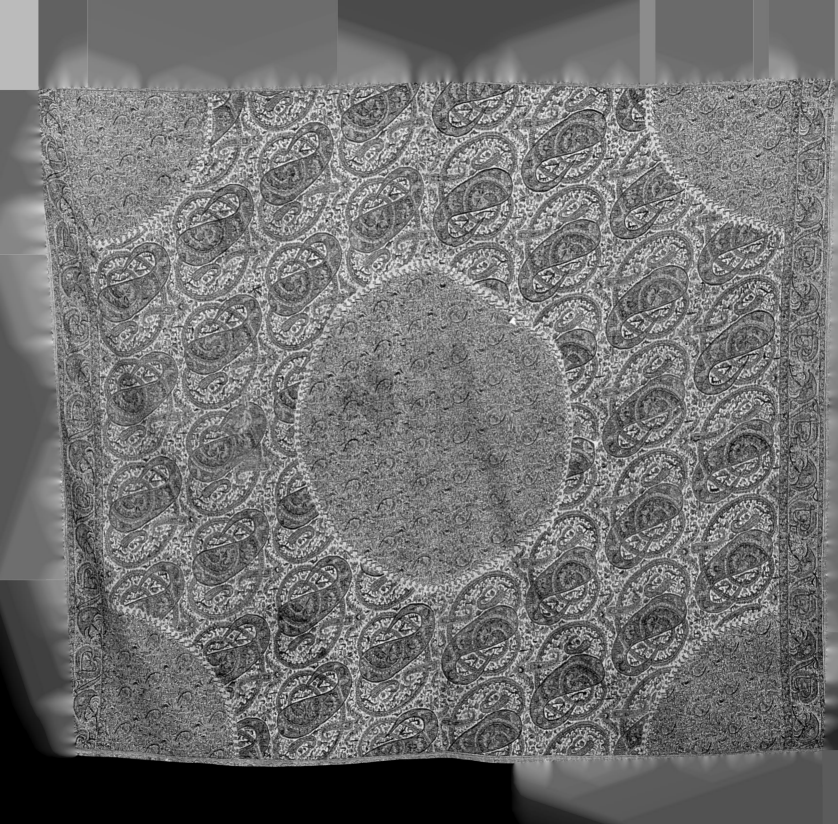

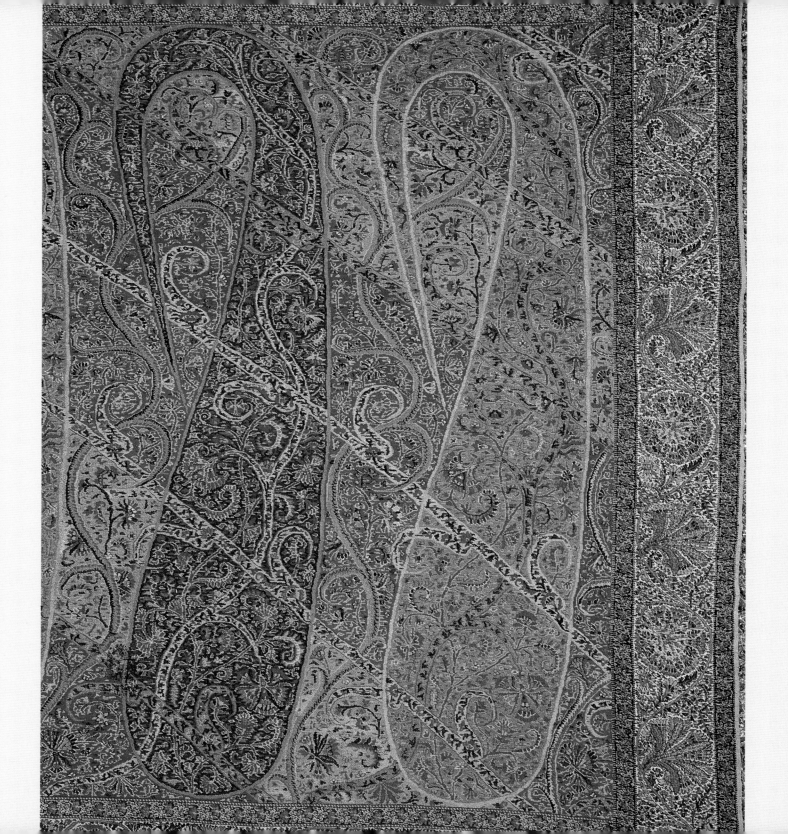

WRAPPED IN SHAWL

Shal, an Indo-Persian word; *dhussa*, a Hindi and Punjabi word for rough woollen *chadar* or covering; and *paramnaram*, a hybrid word used by Mughal emperor Akbar for the softest variety are terms used for the shawl—the long, rectangular woollen fabric used as a drape throughout the history of Indian costumes. In India shawls were made of wool, silk or cotton. The choice of material depended on the climate of the user's area, the status of the user and, of course, the occasion for which it would have been worn.

Since the thrust here is on pashmina, woollen shawls will be discussed in detail. Archaeological and literary examples indicate the antiquity of shawls, the style of wearing them, their size, and the development of patterns and ornamental techniques.

Men and women both used shawls as a drape or a warp as is evidenced from Harappan stone sculptures, mediaeval miniature paintings, and later-period oil paintings. From this evidence, it appears that there were two popular style of wearing the shawl: first, to wrap the shawl under the right arm and cover only the left shoulder. Two, the shawl is wrapped from the left to the right shoulder in such a manner that it covers both the shoulders. Apart from these popular styles, one more fashion, prevalent among Afghanis and Europeans, has the square shawls being worn instead of the regular, rectangular ones. The square shawls were folded diagonally and worn around both the shoulders such that the triangular fold rested on the back and both the ends hung over the shoulder on the front. The most significant and detailed information regarding how shawls were worn are found in Abul Fazl's *Ain-i-Akbari:* 'People were using the shawl by folding it four times and Akbar introduced the style of wearing the shawl without a fold just over the shoulder.' Akbar also wore the *do-shalla* style: the stitching of two identical shawls back to back, so that from both sides the shawl looks the same and beautiful. The concept of the double shawl got proper shape later in the form of the *do-rukha* around 1860-90, when the embroidered shawl gained much popularity.

The shawl industry of Kashmir was initially a cottage industry; it got imperial status (1586 to 1753) under Akbar. Under him Lahore (Punjab) was one of the leading centres for shawl production. Under the patronage of his successors—Jahangir, Shahjahan and Aurangzeb—the shawl industry grew, and significant changes occurred in the material, dyes and wearing styles, which resulted in the most artistic

FACING PAGE: DETAIL OF LONG SHAWL, KASHMIR, MID-19TH CENTURY.

63

shawls, especially, as regards the floral patterns and in the use of shade and colour. Very few Mughal pieces are housed in various museums all over the world. The early shawl pieces are in the Calico Museum, Ahmedabad; Bharat Kala Bhavan, Varanasi; Victoria and Albert Museum, London; and AEDTA, Paris. The later-period pieces are comparatively numerous and found in the Bharat Kala Bhavan and Calico Museum as well as in the Prince of Wales Museum, Mumbai; City Palace, Jaipur; Salar Jung Museum, Hyderabad; Indian Museum, Calcutta; and the National Museum, New Delhi. Rectangular or square, these *kani* shawls were made in various lengths and widths depending on the size of the loom, the individual's choice and the wearing style. These shawls have a length of 225 cm to 340 cm and a width of 125 cm to 140 cm. The colour schemes and designs vary from one shawl to another as per the requirements of the market and the patrons. Several such features were noticed while studying the shawl collections of various museums, which leads to some general observations:

The initial structure of the shawl was simple, generally plain (an off-white field), occasionally coloured (in maroon, navy blue, green, brown), and with narrow end panels decorated with a row of single flower *botehs* or several rows of *buties*. Good line work, design, and colour were the main attractions of the Mughal pattern. A single flower *boteh* illustrating the flower, bud and leaves with bases is the common feature of the early shawls. Generally poppy / lily / rose were the flowers which along with curved angular leaves made the *boteh* design. The National Museum collection of shawls illustrates *botehs*, several rows of *buties* on the end panels, and staggered lines all over the field. Usually subdued, soft colours were used for making fine designs on end panels, while beautiful narrow *hashias* illustrated the floral creeper.

After the Mughals, Afghans ruled Kashmir from 1753 to 1819 and Kashmiri shawls of this period became popular outside the Indian market. The most important feature of this period was the introduction of the new square shawl smaller than the earlier rectangular shawl. These were made for Afghani and European markets. A number of new designs were introduced and the most important pattern was the *kalka boteh,* which took shape from the floral *boteh*. Other patterns include mosaic decoration on the *boteh*, the rose-top *boteh*, the depiction of ten *botehs* on the end panel, a zigzag pattern all over the field, and the small size *coif boteh*. Out of all these, the most important piece is the *zari*-woven end panel of the plain mosaic shawl—the only one of its kind known so far. As far as design is concerned, several new experiments and variations were carried out during this period.

In 1819 under the leadership of Ranjeet Singh, Kashmir became a part of the Sikh kingdom and remained so till 1846. During this period, several European travellers visited India and recorded valuable accounts. Some French and British officials who worked with Ranjeet Singh provided a lot of information through letters. The emperor took keen interest, according to accounts, and his direct supervision gave new life to the industry. Soon the shawl became one of the most popular items for export to France and England. Apart from woven shawls, embroidered ones gained popularity. Therefore, the Indian and international markets saw woven and embroidered shawls created with soft quality wool with new designs. Most shawls of this period had intricate patterns. A few most popular motifs were the stylised *kalka boteh* in various sizes, the hooked vine, fool's cap, cypress tree, star, and the architectural designs. Apart from shawls the *do-shalla* also appeared during this period. Basically, it was made in pieces that were later stitched together around the square centrepiece. In the beginning, the centrepieces of these *do-shallas* were plain, but later they were embroidered with a pattern similar to that on the field. Bright colours like red, black, and green were often found.

The Dogra rulers came around 1846 and ruled Kashmir till 1877. The main advances were in technical development, the introduction of chemical dyes, and Jacquard looms. The patterns of the Sikh period shawl continued into the Dogra period shawls too. But European motifs and colour schemes were reflected in Kashmir mosaic items. The main changes came with the use of vibrant colours, floral patterns, *jal*-type patterns, the introduction of a special technique for making reversible or *do-rukha* shawls by weaving and embroidery and the popularity of especially ordered embroidered shawls, spreads, and *rumals*.

Therefore, the period between the seventeenth and the nineteenth centuries is important, giving lots of information regarding fashion, the economic and commercial conditions, and the technical development of the shawl industry. So far as the National Museum collection is concerned it has a rich variety of shawls: the plain *matan;* zigzag, chequered or staged lined pattern decorated all over the field with an ornamental end panel frame; shawls illustrating a single row of *boteh* or mosaic *botehs; tus* and good quality pashmina*s*. The most noteworthy piece in the collection is the *zari*-woven shawl and those which show the influence of European pattern shawls, which were especially created for the international market.

GUIDE:

b = *boteh*; b.g. = background; f = full; h = *hashia*; h.e.p. = height of end panel; p = pattern

'Single poppy' shawl

MUGHAL, 17TH CENTURY, PASHMINA, TWILL TAPESTRY
TECHNIQUE
COLOUR: OFF-WHITE (B.G.), MAROON, PINK, YELLOW,
GRAYISH GREEN (PATTERN)
SIZE: 13.5 CM (H.E.P.); 11 CM (B); 1 x 1.5 CM (H);
256.7 x 132.5 CM (F)

From the early eighteenth century, floral patterns such as that of the poppy, iris, lily, and rose frequently appeared on silk brocades, printed cotton and woollen shawls. Among these floral motifs the 'single poppy *boteh*' was the most popular, appearing in Mughal textiles, paintings, borders of manuscripts, Mughal architecture, in metal ware utility objects, arms, armours and decorative art objects. The 'single poppy *boteh*' depiction on the end panel of this plain off-white pashmina shawl is an excellent example of the early Mughal textile. A row of twenty-one 'single poppy *boteh*', worked in a wavy formation having four-petal flowers, an irregular, carved stem, buds, roots and curved leaves makes for a balanced *boteh* with attractive colour combinations. The narrow vertical and horizontal *hashias* illustrate the meandering vine motif. A similar off-white shawl is in the Bharat Kala Bhavan, Varanasi. Both these shawls have similar colour treatment, line work, and composition and may belong to the same loom.

Shawl with shades

MUGHAL, 17TH CENTURY, FINE PASHMINA, TWILL
TAPESTRY TECHNIQUE
COLOUR: GREEN (B.G.), MAROON, LIGHT GREEN,
YELLOW, BLUE (P)
SIZE: 17 CM (H.E.P); 13 CM (B); 1.5 x 1.5 CM (H);
332.3 x 138.4 CM (F)

This plain superfine pashmina shawl is an extraordinary example of shades created with a single colour. It reminds one of Moorcroft's account about the Indian dyer's skill in dyeing woollen shawls during the Mughal period in more than 300 colours and shades (for details see Chapter 2). Although this statement appears exaggerated, this shawl shows that high quality dyeing skills were in evidence during the late seventeenth century also. On the brilliant olive green plain shawl, the end panel background in a lighter shade creates a superb demonstration of the dyer's skill. On the light coloured end panel fifteen delicately crafted floral *boteh* having maroon flowers with slightly darker green leaves increase attractiveness. The *boteh* becomes narrow as it grows upwards, and the stylised roots from where the *boteh* starts are based on Chinese ideograms—a common motif of seventeenth-century textiles. Both the *hashias* depicts floral creepers on a blue background. Depiction of floral *botehs* at equal distances makes the end panel impressive. Such *botehs* can be noticed in early Deccani miniature paintings of the seventeenth-eighteenth century rulers of the Deccan.

Mughal buti shawl

MUGHAL, 17TH CENTURY, FINE PASHMINA, TWILL
TAPESTRY TECHNIQUE.
COLOUR: GREY (B.G.), MAROON, PINK, YELLOW,
WHITE, GREEN (P)
SIZE: 17.5 CM (H.E.P); 2 CM (BUTI); 0.8 x 1 CM (H);
320 x 133 CM (F)

Apart from the single poppy floral *boteh,* several rows
of *buties* on the end panel form another variety of the
Mughal floral pattern. The plain grey field of the
shawl has an artistic end panel, which illustrates the
composition of smaller size 'winged leaf' *buties*
arranged in seven rows within the *hashia* frame.
Systematically arranged winged leaf motifs have *buties*
slightly tilted towards one direction, which is
beautifully decorated with a blossoming pink rose
with dark red outlines. The long sweeping branches
and crocus flowers are woven on both the *hashias* on
the white background.

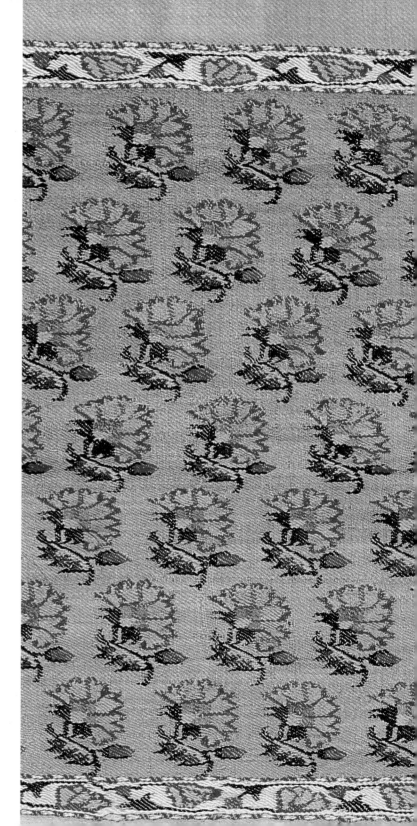

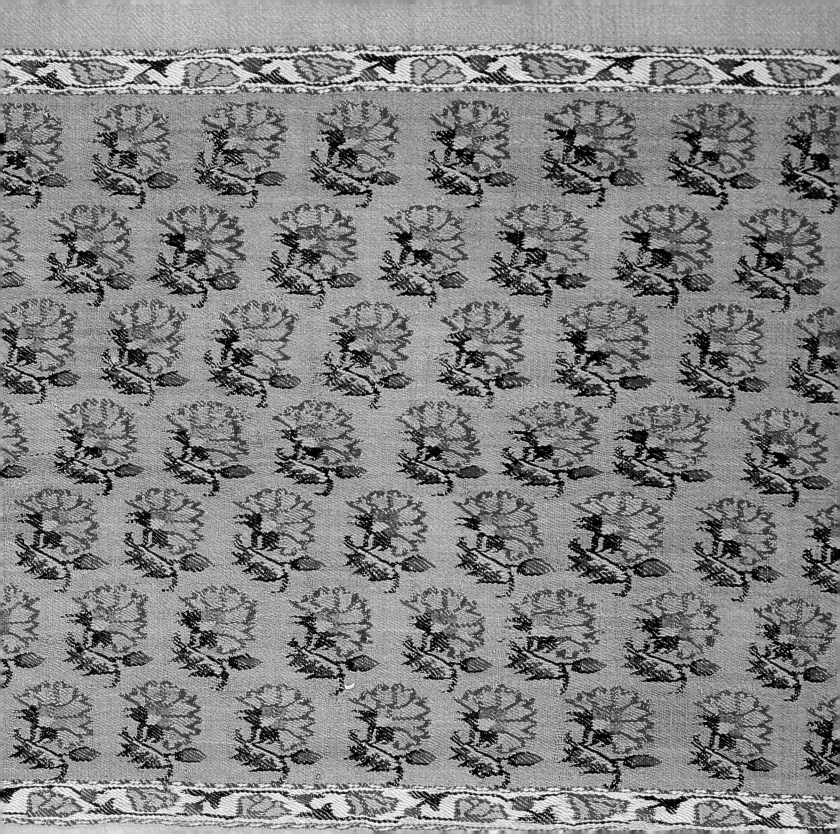

Shawl with rare pattern

MUGHAL, 18TH CENTURY, PASHMINA, TWILL TAPESTRY
TECHNIQUE
COLOUR: OFF-WHITE (B.G.), MAROON, PINK, YELLOW,
BRIGHT YELLOW, PEACH (P)
SIZE: 17 CM (H.E.P); 3 CM (B); 1.3 x 1.8 CM (H);
300 x 127 CM (F)

An attractive design of staggered short lines in navy blue on the entire field of this shawl is a rare example of early shawl work. According to Frank Ames only one more type of this shawl is in the French collection, although the National Museum has more than one similar kind of shawl. The end panel depicts five systematically arranged rows of rose tulip *buties*. The three-flower rose tulip *buti* has Chinese ideogram roots with pointed leaves on either side of flowers—a perfect balancing act. Both the *hashias* portray the floral creeper pattern, but the vertical *hashia* is wider than the horizontal *hashia*.

FACING PAGE

Merged coif boteh shawl

1810-30, AFGHAN, KASHMIR, PASHMINA, TWILL TAPESTRY TECHNIQUE
COLOUR: OFF-WHITE (B.G.), GREY, MAROON, YELLOW, BLUE, BROWN (P)
SIZE: 26 CM (H.E.P.); 7.5 CM (B); 1.7 x 1.7 CM (H); 315 x 137 CM (F)

Three rows of small *coif boteh* on the end panel of this shawl are a fine example of early nineteenth-century work. This *coif boteh* is a new development in which *coif* and *boteh* have merged. Here, the *boteh* has a composition of a few flowers, starting from a small, stylised mound with two leafy fronds supporting it. The right leaf supports the *boteh's* cone of flowers while the left supports the rising arched raceme. Later, the raceme developed to envelop the *boteh*. Between the pair of *coif botehs* at the base, a *buti* is woven. This appears to be an early style of the *coif boteh*, smaller as compared to the later-period. Both *hashias* are equal in size and illustrate the floral creeper.

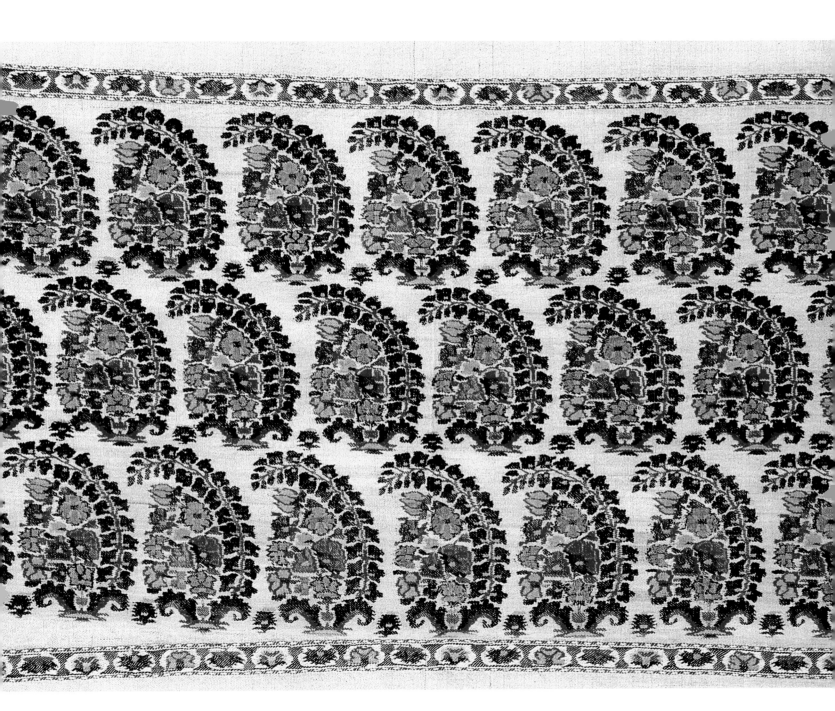

71

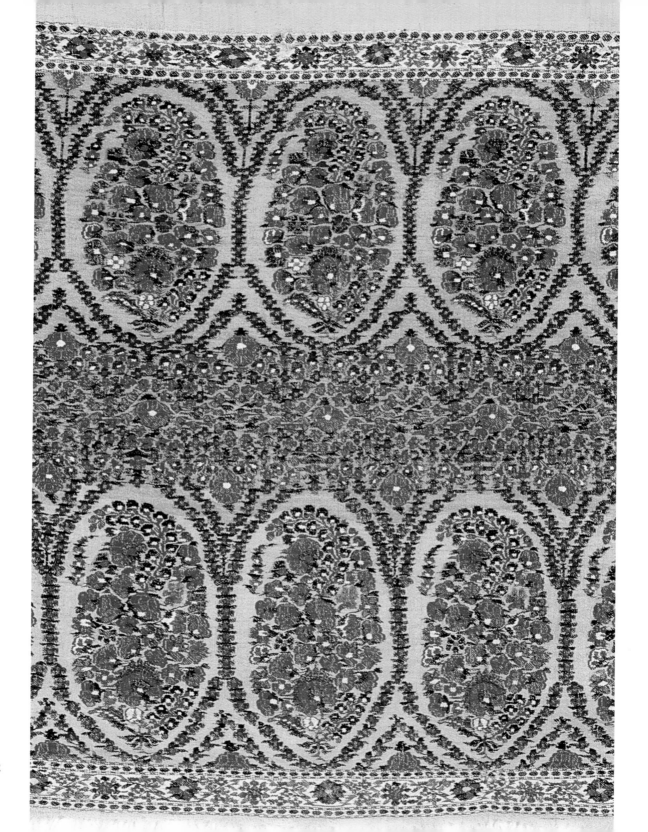

72

European style shawl

1810-30, PASHMINA, KASHMIR, LOOM WOVEN

COLOUR: DEEP YELLOW (B.G.), MAROON, BLUE, WHITE, GREY (P)

SIZE: 40 CM (H.E.P.); 12.5 CM (B); 3 x 3 CM (H); 300 x 134 CM (F)

Since 1820, European designs influenced Kashmiri shawls. Many designers and traders from France and England began visiting Kashmir and giving orders to the weavers according to their own designs. Kashmiri shawls were made for their markets. This fine yellow pashmina plain shawl illustrates two rows of small *kalka botehs* within oval frames arranged in a compartment format, each row made of thirteen *botehs*. Densely composed, these *kalka botehs* have a small tip that tilts to the left and a small additional garland depiction near the tip. The area between the rows of *botehs* is decorated with a floral creeper. The double-row *botehs* within an oval frame appear to be a European influence.

The chevron shawl

AFGHAN PERIOD, 18TH CENTURY, KASHMIR, PASHMINA, LOOM WOVEN
COLOUR: BLUE, WHITE AND MAROON ON THE ENTIRE SHAWL AND PATTERN
SIZE: 31 CM (H.E.P.); 1.7 X 2.5 CM (H); 276 X 136 CM (F)

The most popular motif of Persian art is chevron, which symbolises flowing water. To create this impression, the zigzag patterns were closely woven. Only a few shawls and *rumals* have been found with this motif. This beautiful shawl illustrates the zigzag pattern all over the field in blue and white. With the help of two different sizes of the zigzag pattern, the artist has succeed in creating the difference between the field and the end panel. The field has

74

a broad zigzag pattern while the end panel has a smaller zigzag design. Both *hashias* have also been done in a similar fashion, but the change in direction and colour adds to the beauty. Probably such shawls were especially made for the Afghan market.

Shawl with inscriptions

AFGHAN PERIOD, 1805-25, KASHMIR, PASHMINA, LOOM WOVEN
COLOUR: MAROON (B.G.); BLUE, GREY, YELLOW, MAROON, PINK, WHITE (P)
SIZE: 32 CM (H.E.P.); 28 CM (B);1.6 x 2 CM (H); 382 x 135 CM (F)

The rich maroon field of this shawl has a unique feature: a small inscription plaque woven in the *hashia* along with the strawberry bent tip and the rose pattern floral creeper running alternately all around the *hashia*. Usually, inscriptions were embroidered in some of the later period shawls. In this shawl, however, the inscription is woven in the *hashia* with uniform lettering—remarkable! A heavy ornate end panel illustrates ten closely composed floral *botehs*; between two *botehs* at the base is a small flower motif hanging on a bird motif on either side. The floral *boteh* starts from the vase placed on a flat dish. It has a radial arrangement becoming narrower as it grows upwards with a fully blossomed rose on the top. There is a slight bend towards the left of the *boteh* and a garland is woven close to the *boteh*'s top to balance the composition.

Bright blue shawl

AFGHAN PERIOD, 1805-25, KASHMIR, PASHMINA,
LOOM WOVEN
COLOUR: BLUE (B.G.), MAROON, YELLOW,
GRAYISH GREEN, PINK, (P)
SIZE: 32 (H.E.P.); 28.5 CM (B); 1.5 x 2 CM (H);
304 x 135 CM (F)

Bright blue is yet another colour often found in Mughal textiles. This good quality blue shawl illustrates a colourful composition of ten elongated *botehs* on the broad end panel within the *hashia* frame. These *botehs,* which start from the vase placed on a flat back, are composed of tiny flowers in a radial arrangement with a flower on top. An additional garland in the form of a floral *boteh* is at the top of the *boteh*. A narrow meandering vine creeper is on both the *hashia*. Twisted fringes add grace.

FACING PAGE

19th-century shawl

EARLY 19TH CENTURY, KASHMIR, PASHMINA, LOOM WOVEN
COLOUR: MAROON (B.G.), YELLOW, BLUE, PINK (P)

A similar kind of treatment in floral *boteh* composition is seen on this maroon pashmina shawl, which has a row of ten floral *botehs* on the end panel within the *hashia* frame. The floral *boteh* is full of small flowers, creepers, and leaves with full-blossomed flowers on the top. Two additional floral garlands are on the top curved towards the left. They are closer to the *kalka boteh* structure.

Pashmina with zari

KASHMIR, 1830-50, PASHMINA AND ZARI, LOOM WOVEN
COLOUR: MAROON RED (B.G.), MAROON, PINK, BLUE, GREY (P)
SIZE: 55 CM (H.E.P.); 40 CM (B); 5 x 5.2 CM (H); 264 x 140 CM (F)

Wool weaving with silk is a common feature but pashmina woven with *zari* is rare and extraordinary. This plain maroon red pashmina shawl has an extraordinary end panel, which is magnificently woven with gold *zari* thread. Ten elongated *botehs* are woven with extra weft *zari* thread in something like the Pathani style of brocade weaving. This *zari* shawl becomes more significant in the light of the reference in *Ain-i-Akbari*, where the book talks about *kalabatu* work, saying 'the designs seem to have been brocaded with gold wire'. However, woollen shawls woven with *zari* are not known in any other collection so far. This shawl does not belong to the Mughal period, however, it shows the continuity of traditional *zari* weaving with wool, which was specially crafted as a gift for the Brahmins. The fully decorated *boteh* depicts floral motifs and small flowers near the tip are also woven, which gives the impression that these flowers were dropping from the tip. The *boteh* starts from the stem and narrows as it grows upwards; the curved tip turns towards the left. Near the curve of the *boteh,* there are two more flower garlands. In between the pair of *botehs* at the base is a small floral plant surrounded by a leaf-like arch. Both the broad *hashias* illustrate a full-blossomed flower and creeper, the only difference is that the horizontal one is woven and the vertical *hashia* is stitched. The second panel depicts a four-flower motif within a square frame. A little appliqué work has been done on the corner of the field near the end panel frame, which illustrates the *kalka boteh* woven separately and stitched on to the field.

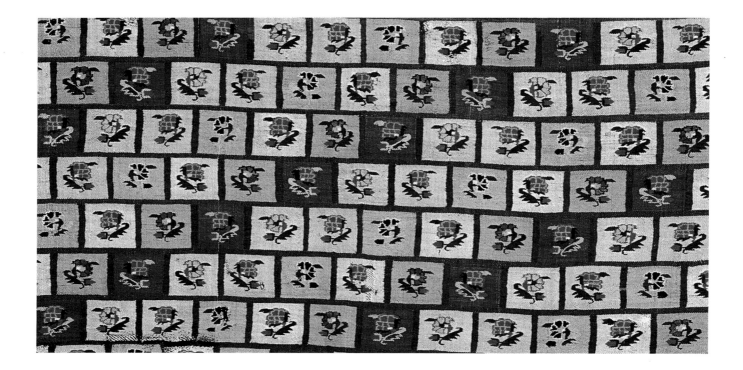

The checkerboard shawl

1815-35, KASHMIR, PASHMINA, SILK, TWILL TAPESTRY TECHNIQUE
COLOUR: PALE BLUE, YELLOW, (PATTERN): MAROON, PINK, WHITE, YELLOW
SIZE: 33.5 CM (H.E.P.); 30 CM (B); 1.5 x 2 CM (H); 320 x 135 CM (F)

Plain or staggered lines appear on the field of early Kashmiri shawls. In the early nineteenth century, the plain field started with little ornamentation and slowly the plain fields of the shawl were replaced by heavy ornamentation on the border or all over the field. In this group the most important piece has a checkerboard pattern over the field and elongated *botehs* on the end panel. The pattern depicts a winged leaf flower *buti* alternately in maroon and blue on a background of three different colours. Two such rows of *buties* are woven in opposite directions. The end panel illustrates ten elongated *botehs* that have been given a treatment similar to the three earlier shawls, but here these are woven in compartments on two different backgrounds. The only interesting feature of this *boteh*'s base is the floral cross decoration without a vase. However, in the usual depiction, the floral cross appears on the vase and is placed on a flat dish. The end panel pattern with a field decoration makes this nineteenth-century shawl an important work of art from the design point of view.

80

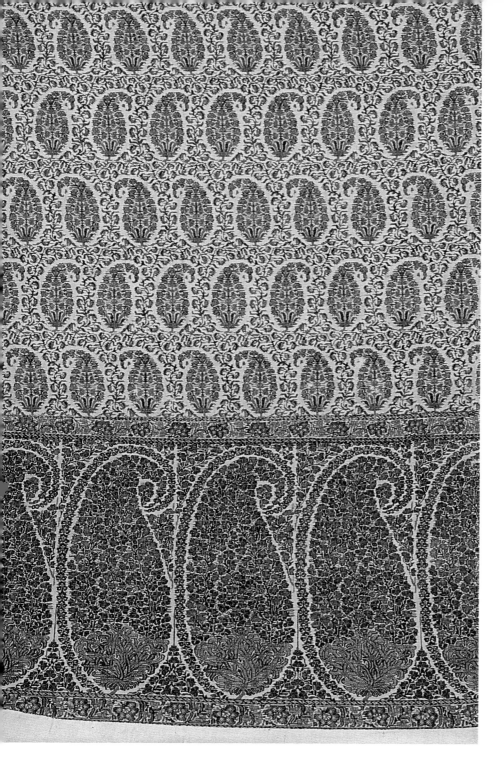

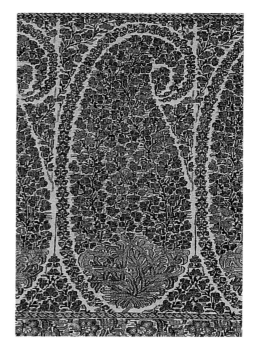

Shawl with ornamented matan

AFGHAN, 1810-40, KASHMIR, PASHMINA,
LOOM WOVEN
COLOUR: OFF-WHITE (B.G.), BLUE, MAROON,
GREYISH GREEN, PINK (P)
SIZE: 36 CM (H.E.P.); 29 CM (B);
3 x 3 CM (H); 308 x 132 CM (F)

Around the mid-eighteenth century the
field of the shawl was designed so that the
small un-worked ground portion became a
part of it. The fully designed field of this
long shawl shows a small *kalka* motif
surmounted by a densely woven creeper
pattern. The remaining ground portion
makes the oval frame. The end panel

depicts nine large *coif botehs* with a small stem-type arrangement. The entire *boteh* is woven with tiny flowers while the lower portion has a honeybee-type depiction of branches and flowers. A long additional garland goes from the base to the curve of the *kalka boteh,* which becomes a part of the main *kalka boteh.* Both vertical and horizontal *hashias* are of similar size and woven with a floral creeper pattern.

19th-century pashmina

EARLY 19TH CENTURY, KASHMIR, PASHMINA, LOOM WOVEN
COLOUR: OFF WHITE (B.G.), BLUE, MAROON, PINK (P)

A similar kind of colour treatment has been given while ornamenting the *matan* and end panel of this fine pashmina shawl. The off-white background *matan* is fully ornamented with small *kalka buties* and nine large *kalka botehs* are on the end panel. It appears that this shawl and the earlier one have been made from same loom.

The hooked vine pattern

SIKH PERIOD, 1830-50, PASHMINA, LOOM WOVEN
COLOUR: RED (B.G.), BLUE, GREY, YELLOW, PINK (P)
SIZE: 40 CM (H.E.P.); 30 CM (B); 4.5 X 4 CM (H);
300 X 137CM (F)

The decorated *matan* of this long maroon shawl has an ornamented end panel depicting eight elongated *botehs* arranged in a compartment divided by a hooked vine pattern. The entire field of the shawl illustrates diagonally arranged small *kalka buties* in white and pink alternately. They are surrounded by an angular outline of sky blue flowers with small leaves in the lower portion that make the *kalka* pattern charming. The end panel illustrates the straight floral *boteh* that starts from a small stem, narrowing as it grows up and ends in a nice curved tip. The *boteh's* inner structure depicts the leaf-type design arranged with a hooked vine in the lower portion. In between, the pinecone motif of the *boteh* is woven in two colours: yellow and pink and surrounded by three layers of sky-blue angular flowers. Both the *hashias* are done with a full-blossomed flower creeper and a *boteh* motif flower. This *boteh's* composition appears to be the inspiration behind Moorcroft's shawl design. He had prepared various designs during his stay in India and sent them back to London. Only eight of these are known so far. These eight drawings are in the Metropolitan Museum of Art, New York. John Irwin and other scholars have published them.

The European bouquet style

AFGHAN PERIOD, 1820-40, PASHMINA, TWILL TAPESTRY
TECHNIQUE
COLOUR: ORANGISH PEACH (B.G.), BLUE, MAROON,
YELLOW, BROWN, YELLOW (P)
SIZE: 33.5 CM (H.E.P.); 25.5 CM (B);
1 x 3.5 CM (H); 280 x 131.5 CM (F)

The orange-peach field of this shawl is decorated with small *buties* in a symmetrical manner. The European-style bouquet ornamentation is at the corners along with a floral creeper pattern. The highly decorated end panel illustrates ten big *botehs*, which grow from a vase placed on a flat dish, and turn left at the top. The angular floral arrangement of vase, dish, leaves, and flowers become a part of the complete *kalka boteh*. The inner portion of the *boteh* is composed of small blue angular flowers arranged in a row of five branches on either side. A small additional garland on the top is also a part of the *boteh* composition. At the base, between two *botehs*, is a plant whose leaves and branches go down. A narrow end panel frame depicts a floral creeper and fringe gates depict long, multi-coloured stripes embroidered with floral *buties* in purple, yellow and brown under an arch, which appears to be a later addition.

The simple shawl FACING PAGE TOP

1810-30, PASHMINA, TWILL TAPESTRY TECHNIQUE
COLOUR: OFF-WHITE (B.G.), MAROON, BLUE, PINK,
YELLOW (P)
SIZE: 6 CM (B); 0.7 x 1.7 CM (H); 230 x 125 CM (F)

Shawls with less complex patterns were made around the middle of the eighteenth century. Probably they were especially prepared for some special market. This off-white shawl illustrates small floral *buties* arranged all over in a row. These delicately crafted floral *botehs* are a nice composition of tiny flowers, slightly bigger

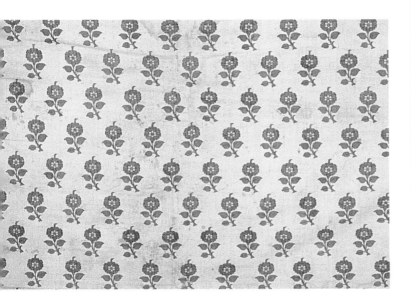

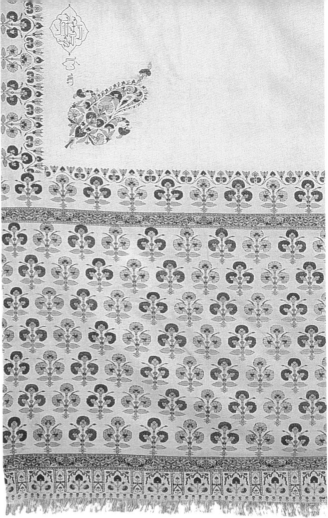

leaves, and a stem. Both the *hashias* have different designs; even these are woven separately and stitched on the shawl. The early style of flower treatment, the symmetric row, the use of minimum colour, and the selection of soft pashmina gives the impression that this piece has been made for the European market, although the artist has maintained the Mughal style of design. In fact, the cloth appears like dress material given the shape of a shawl by adding two *hashias* and a piece of plain cloth at the horizontal edge.

Plain matan shawl

LATE 19TH CENTURY, KASHMIR, PASHMINA, LOOM WOVEN
COLOUR: OFF-WHITE (B.G.), MAROON, BLUE, GREEN,
YELLOW, BLACK, PURPLE (P)
SIZE: 49 CM (H.E.P.); 6 CM (B); 2.7 CM (H);
210 x 134 CM (F)

Broad end panels having an additional border near the field with a corner *boteh* make this plain *matan* shawl a good example of nineteenth-century work. The end panel depicts small, stylised floral *botehs* composed of three half-blossomed flowers, leaves, buds and roots, reminiscent of the trefoil pattern often seen in textiles, and looking more colourful when arranged in two colours. The absence of a vertical *hashia*, a broad, ornamented horizontal *hashia*, and an additional narrow border at the edge of the lower horizontal *hashia* are the other important features. The lower *hashia* is divided into square compartments, is ornate with an arched pattern, and has a flower *boteh* like the one on the field. A short inscription is embroidered on the edge within the oblong frame.

Pashmina with restrained colours

19TH CENTURY, KASHMIR, PASHMINA, LOOM-WOVEN
COLOUR: OFF-WHITE (B.G.), BLUE, MAROON (P)

The design in this shawl is similar to the earlier shawl, but fewer colours make it an attractive piece. Here the plain field shawl has a broad decorated end panel depicting eight *kalka botehs*; an additional border towards the *matan* also depicts the *kalka buties*. Straight *kalka botehs* and a row of tilted *kalka buties* in the opposite direction are a striking feature of this shawl.

88

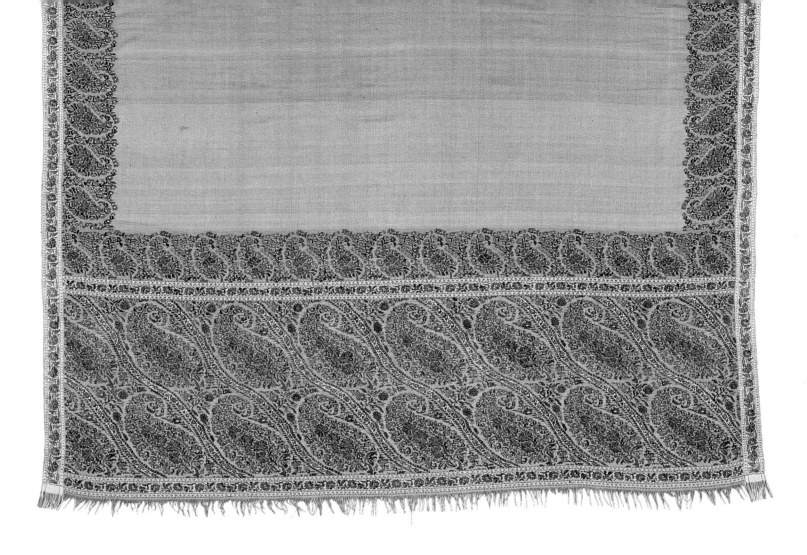

A green shawl

1825-50, Kashmir, pashmina, loom woven
Colour: Green (b.g.), blue, maroon, yellow (p)

A similar design has been used for decorating this green pashmina shawl. A plain *matan* has a *kalka buti* border near the end panel on the field and a double row of *kalka botehs* on the end panel. They are beautifully woven diagonally but in the same direction. They are then divided by a *hashia* having a floral creeper on a white background.

An export shawl

AFGHAN PERIOD, 1810-30, PASHMINA,
KASHMIR, TWILL TAPESTRY TECHNIQUE
COLOUR: RED (B.G.), DARK, LIGHT BLUE,
PINK, GREY, YELLOW (P)
SIZE: 5 CM (B); 0.6 CM (H); 264 X 140 CM (F)

Full-blossomed flower *botehs* arranged in a zigzag all over the field on a red background make this shawl attractive. Two rows of flowers are woven in an opposite direction, which create the zigzag pattern. The most important feature of this *boteh* is the full-blossomed flower decorated with a double row of petals in maroon and blue, a small root base and curved leaves. Its narrow horizontal *hashia* depicts a small, segregated leaf design, reminiscent of a mosaic leaf motif, on a grey-white background. It appears that this type of design on a shawl cloth was made especially for export.

90

Sikh period do-shalla

DETAIL IN NEXT PAGE

LONG SHAWL, SIKH PERIOD, 1840-60,
PASHMINA, LOOM WOVEN
COLOUR: RED, OFF-WHITE, GREEN, YELLOW,
PINK (B.G. & P), BLUE (CENTRE)
SIZE: 82 (H.E.P.); 19 (DHORA);
13 (VERTICAL H); 320 x 146 CM (F)

Long *kalka botehs*, hooked vine, crescent, star, boat, birds, animals are some motifs used during the Sikh period of *do-shalla* shawls. Some features are well presented in this shawl such as long end panels, *hashias*, field ornamentation and a plain blue centre with the border pattern all over. The end panel depicts a pair of long *kalka boteh* having a deep curved tip; the centre shows a long pine motif above the horizontal *hashias*. It also has an arched area surrounded by natural vegetation, a peacock and a star-shaped pond. The entire panel is so densely decorated that the motifs twine with each other forming a new design. The vertical *hashia* is broad and depicts the *kalka*, leaves and other motifs with a narrow, floral creeper border. An extra border treats the motifs similarly.

91

The new shawl

LONG SHAWL, SIKH PERIOD, 1830-50, PASHMINA
COLOUR: LIGHT GREEN (B.G.), BLACK, GREEN,
OFF-WHITE, RED, YELLOW, PINK (P)
SIZE: 125 CM (HEIGHT OF LONG HORIZONTAL
PANEL); 154 x 344 CM (F)

Under Sikh rule, Maharaja Ranjeet Singh took keen interest and several new experiments in composition, motifs, and colour appeared on Kashmiri shawls. Apart from the *matan*, end panel, and *hashia*, new elements such as the *tanjir* (lateral border ornament), the *dhora* (running ornament surrounding the field), long vertical *hashias*, a narrow plain fringe gate, and fringes were introduced. This light green background shawl with intricate patterns in coloured, arched compartments—for example, long *kalka botehs* having a hooked vine, flowering plant, and stripes—illustrates different types of stylised trees. The colours keep changing subtly from red to brown to pink as do the widths of the stripes into which the motifs are placed. A green square that occupies the centre is richly patterned with a floral creeper. The vertical *hashia* that runs the whole length of the shawl contains a continuous pattern of floral creepers and leafy motifs. The narrow fringe gates are black, green, off-white, red and yellow.

Four-coloured khatraaz shawl

KHATRAAZ SHAWL, LATE 19TH CENTURY, (1850-70),
KASHMIR, PASHMINA, LOOM WOVEN
COLOUR: YELLOW, GREEN, OFF-WHITE, ALTERNATING BLUE
AND MAROON STRIPES DIVIDE EACH STRIPE
SIZE: 8.5 CM (STRIPES); 270 X 123 CM (F)

Apart from the design, one more style can be notice in the later period shawls, that of multicoloured long shawls having a *khatraaz* design on the complete field. Some early period *khatraaz* shawls illustrate the *hashia* motif in a colourful manner. Initially the *khatraaz* fabric was used as a dress material; some paintings show the *choga* being made of a *khatraaz*-type fabric. Later, these were used as a shawl. This four-coloured *khatraaz* shawl having vertical stripes divided by a narrow maroon border depicts small *buties* arranged in a row. The main vertical stripes depict a blossoming flower surrounded by two *kalka buties* in opposite direction, three-flower patterns, and leaf motifs that are around the centre floral *buties*. The use of yellow, green, off-white, blue and maroon in the most balanced form makes the shawl charming.

94

The striped khatraaz

LAST QUARTER OF THE 19TH CENTURY,
PASHMINA, LOOM WOVEN
COLOUR: YELLOW, MAROON, WHITE, GREEN,
BLUE ALTERNATELY USED
SIZE: 8 TO 9 CM (S); 255 X 125 CM (F)

This is another good example of the *khatraaz* shawl. It has long vertical, multicoloured stripes in two narrow sizes after broad four-coloured stripes. The narrow stripes are yellow and white, which illustrate flower *buties*. The broad stripes depict the floral creeper, *kalka* and the stylised flower woven all over the field in multicolour. A small, plain maroon portion is a later addition. It could be dress material, but by adding the plain cloth at the horizontal end and putting the piping on vertical edges, the cloth has been given the shape of a shawl.

FOLLOWING PAGES 96-97: SHAWL, C. 1870-90, KASHMIR,
PASHMINA, WOVEN, 290 X 140 CM (F)

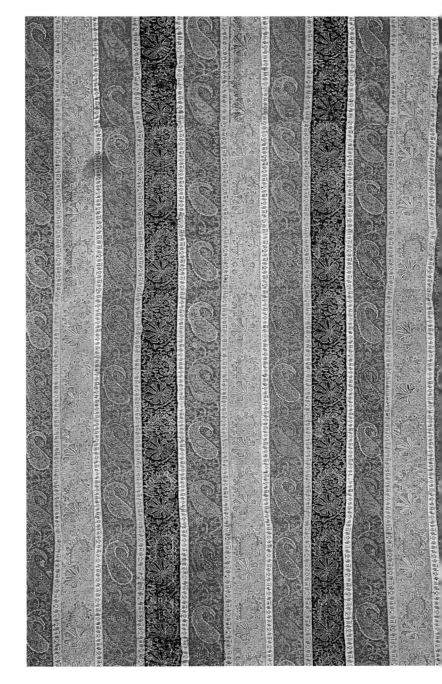

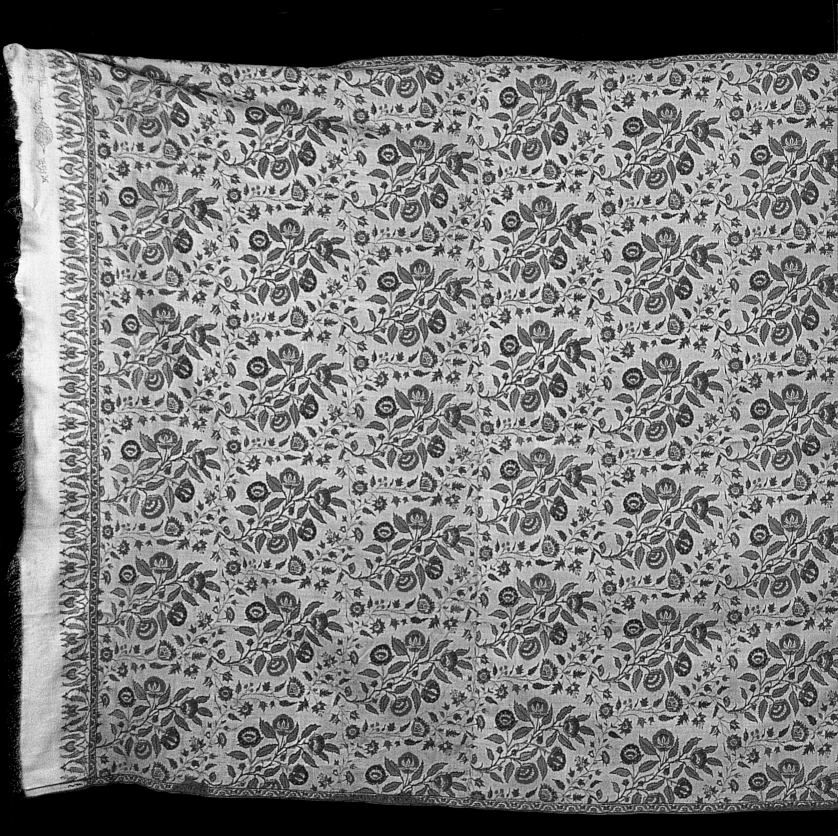

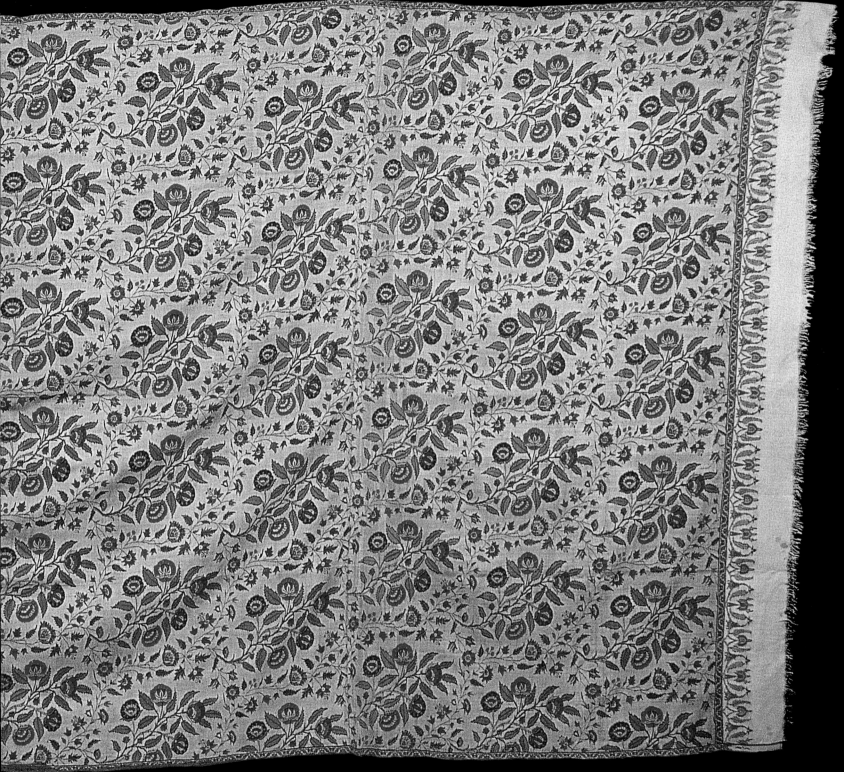

Double-shade shawl

DOGRA PERIOD, LATE 19TH CENTURY,
PASHMINA, KASHMIR
COLOUR: DOUBLE SHADE OF PINK AND
BROWN (B.G.), PINK, GREEN, PURPLE,
RED, BLACK, YELLOW (P)
SIZE: 21.5 CM (B); 290 x 140 CM (F)

The last phase of royal patronage for the Kashmiri shawls came under the Dogra rulers (1846-1877). This was the period of European influence as demand for such material increased in the European market. The influence of the colour scheme, the floral pattern, and its composition can be noticed on this shawl. With the use of pink and off-white threads, this shawl gave a double-shade effect, which makes it more attractive and colourful. The entire field of this shawl is decorated with *boteh,* which is a bunch of blossoming flowers, segregated leaves, and buds woven diagonally to give a wave-like effect to the motif. Additional creepers having elongated leaves, different from the field pattern, are woven towards the end panel and a small inscription is embroidered at the plain end panel. Both the *hashias* depict floral creepers. It appears to be dress material converted into a shawl as its *hashias* and end panels have been joined later.

The Ramanami shawl

DOGRA PERIOD, LAST QUARTER OF 19TH CENTURY, KASHMIR, LOOM WOVEN
COLOUR: LIGHT GREEN (B.G.), BRIGHT PINK, BLUE, ORANGISH YELLOW, GREEN, BROWN (P)
SIZE: 22 CM (H.E.P); 1.5 CM (H.H); 16 CM (B); 4.3 CM (FRINGE GATE); 307 X 133 CM (F)

A long, light green Ramanami shawl is a fine example of an inscribed shawl. It is surrounded by a floral *hashia*, ornamental end panels and a fringe gate. The field is divided into thirty rectangular panels arranged in six rows each. These panels are woven with inscribed alternately the various names of godesses, in Bangla and Devanagri scripts in different colours. The end panel is decorated with flower clusters. A narrow horizontal *hashia* on an orange backdrop depicts a floral creeper. *Boteh* motif is inside the field and all around the vertical border. The fringe gate depicts small rectangular compartments having arches on the top and a flower *buti* inside. The use of *tus* or pashmina wool, good colours, designs and fine *kani* weaving resulted in a superb product.Starting with a single row of flower *boteh*, it evolved into the coif, *kalka,* and mosaic patterns.

EMBROIDERING MAGIC: AMLIKAR ARTISTRY

The term *Amlikar* stands for embroidery or ornamental work that is done on the textile surface and which looks like embossing. Around the mid-nineteenth century, the fields of Kashmiri shawls were embroidered so finely that they became fashionable and drew more recognition than *kani* shawls. One of the reasons behind the popularity of *amli* shawl was the heavy tax on *kani* shawls levied by Afghan rulers. Also, an *amli* shawl required little technology and was created in less time so it also gave more creativity and money to the artisan. As a result, magnificent works of art were created, which were not possible through weaving or in *kani* shawls.

Amlikar or *amli* means embroidery; it probably began with the embroidered imitation of a woven shawl and so got the name *amlikar* that means 'to copy.' It appears that *amlikar* shawls initially did not have much embroidery. The imitation of woven patterns in embroidery was done in different areas of the shawls. Incidentally, the National Museum collection has one such example, which shows a row of *kalka boteh* woven

on the end panel frame of a shawl and a similar kind of *kalka boteh* embroidered on the field as a corner *boteh*. But, *amlikar* soon developed its own style and the famous Kashmiri embroidery was born.

HISTORY OF *AMLIKAR*

Kashmiri embroidery came into existence in the early nineteenth century, according to most scholars. They are of the view that 'in 1803 an Armenian agent, Khwaja Yusuf from Constantinople, thought of simulating the *kani* shawl designs and colour combinations with a hand [-held] needle.' This view is based on William Moorcroft's accounts. He further states that 'he achieved this through the skill of a seamster named Ali Baba', who was a Persian expert from Kirman and taught embroidery to Kashmiris. The *amlikar* style was taken up probably during the rule of Kashmir's Afghan governor, Azim Khan. He reintroduced the system of forcible sale of grain at enhanced prices to weavers in addition to the payment of tax. The shawl produced on the loom was taken by the state and the price of grain together with the amount of duty levied on it was recovered from its sales proceeds. This led to a decline in the number of shawl looms in Kashmir.

FACING PAGE: DETAIL OF JAJAM SPREAD, KASHMIR, MID-CENTURY, PASHMINA, WOVEN AND EMBROIDERED, 440 X 117 CM.

This opinion needs reconsideration since embroidery was not introduced in Kashmir in the early nineteenth century. A few significant references to it exist before this period. The most important mention is in the *Ain-i-Akbari* where an entire chapter has been devoted to the shawl. It outlines how 'His Majesty took keen interest in the improvement of this [shawl] sector in four ways.' And while describing the third way, it states the methods used for adorning the shawls; it also mentions *Kasida* and *Zardozi* work among the categories. *Kasida* means 'embroidery' and *Zardozi* is 'a type of embroidery done with *zari* or golden thread.' Akbar established many imperial *karkhanas*; sometimes his *subedars* did the same. These imperial *karkhanas* were set up at the capital and provincial headquarters and in important industrial towns. After Akbar's victory over Punjab in 1585 and Kashmir in 1586, Lahore was one such centre. In these centres workers got patronage, protection and opportunities to make different items: costumes, jewellery, arms and armour. Embroidery was also practised in these centres as is evident by two incidents. The first is the devastating fire that occurred during Akbar's time, in 1579, at one such centre, Fatehpur Sikri, capital of Akbar's empire. The fire destroyed the *Farrashkhana* (private storehouse) where Akbar's most valuable textiles were kept. 'Embroidered pieces' were among items in the list of losses, which proves that embroidery existed during Akbar's period in the *karkhanas*. It is likely that when one or two centres followed the tradition, the other imperial centres may also have done the same. The second is Bernier's travel account of his visit to India in 1663. During his visit to the fort, he writes that he had seen *karkhanas* and embroiderers, adding that 'it was hereditary for an embroiderer's son to be an embroiderer'. This seventeenth-century reference is vital. Moreover, the *rafugar*, who existed since the earliest stage of shawl making, always had a hand in the finishing work. The nimble-fingered seamstresses, called *rafugars,* used to give finishing touches to *Kani* shawls by attaching borders, edgings, reinforcing and retouching the design and the colour. Hence the art of using the needle skilfully on *Kani* existed earlier. The role of the *rafugars* was undeniably important even for *kani* shawls. Therefore, it could be possible that Moorcroft saw Khwaja Yusuf giving a particular shape—which exists today—to embroidered shawls. Yusuf might have had a better idea of the market for the Kashmiri shawl and may have helped weavers and embroiderers work accordingly. His contribution cannot be denied, but the tradition of embroidery existed much before the nineteenth century.

THE *AMLIKAR* PROCESS

William Moorcroft gave a detailed description of woven and embroidered shawls. The shawls were woven plain and were ornamented with embroidery using yarns of silk, wool, and *zari*. Generally fine coloured, staple pashm wool and *zari* threads were used for embroidery. However, silk yarns were used less. These threads were available in the local market, but occasionally better yarn was bought from Amritsar or Mumbai. Before using it, threads were dyed in different colours by private dyers in Kashmir.

After getting the raw material and the woven fabric, different stitches were used for creating motifs. For *amli* work, the first step was the selection of pattern. Professionals called *Naquashband* who were specialists in tracing patterns came next. The pattern was first covered with transparent paper set upon the outlines of the composition and lightly traced with a charcoal twig. The traced lines were permanently defined by perforation with a fine needle. The perforated sheets were placed on the fabric and chalk or charcoal powder rubbed over it. The impression of the design was left on the fabric's surface. Such perforated tracing patterns were stored for use. Moorcroft's description runs thus: 'The cloth intended to receive the pattern is rubbed strongly upon a smooth plank with a piece of highly polished agate or carnelian until it is perfectly even and regular.' To add durability, Arabic gum or oil was added to charcoal or chalk powder. Occasionally, the outlines of the tracings were sharpened with the help of a *kalam*. After tracing the patterns on the surface of the fabric, a variety of stitches were used for the designs. Different names have been assigned to various types of stitches. A few important ones are:

1. The basic stitch is the darn stitch, which *rafugars* often used on *kani* shawls to give finishing touches. Later, the same stitch was used for imitating woven designs on embroidered shawls. It's a kind of running stitch worked over the counted threads on the ground of the fabric in rows to form a pattern. These stitches nipped the loops of the warp threads, the needle penetrating the surface once in a while. When used in embroidery it can be called a form of the parallel darn stitch. G. Watts, in *Art and Crafts of India*, says that the designs produced with this technique revealed the original woven designs in all their fineness.

2. The next most frequently used stitch is the stem stitch. It is used to sharpen the outlines of the design. Normally, this stitch is demarcated by a darker shade so that the depth of the motif becomes clearer. The stitches are done as flat as possible against the ground and the individual threads of the warp are picked up in the stitching.

3. The *sozani* is the next most popular stitch and works on all woollen fabrics. The beauty of this stitch is its delicacy, which lends uniformity to both sides of the fabric and gives, from a distance, a printed effect. *Sozani* is minute work, sometimes a complex design that is embroidered all over and which may take up to three years. Thus, it is expensive. Embroidery threads are always single strands of either silk or staple pashm. The finest *sozani* has three basic stitches—one is a straight line, which can be varied in length, and can be made into a continuous curved line or even small dashes. This is always reinforced with a smaller stitch over it. The second is a simple diamond-shaped outline, which was used for petals and leaves. The third is a filling-up stitch, generally used for completing the larger areas of the motifs. Like the straight line, these small stitches are also reinforced. Often, if the area is large enough, stitches from both sides meet three-fourths of the way through the marked area. To make dots, closer stitches are used. Outline stitches are made after the petals are filled in. In *sozani* most craftsmen make sure that the ground does not show, especially, between the filling up and the outline. This makes *sozani* work special.

4. Sometimes satin, chain, and *watachikan* stitches are used in Kashmiri embroidery. Satin is a filling stitch, which covers motifs with closely worked parallel stitches to form a smooth surface. It is used only for motifs of limited size, as long stitches become loose and untidy when the embroidered article is used. In early Kashmiri embroidery, the chain stitch can be seen as an outlining stitch in the form of a chain of looped stitches. The same stitch is also used as a filling stitch. It can be worked with either a needle or a hook. When the chain stitch is worked with a needle, the thread is held above the cloth, the loop is wound round the tip of the needle and secured by the flowing stitch. When filling with the chain stitch, consecutive rows are set close together and a plain effect obtained by using a single colour. A shaded effect is given by using different coloured threads in intermittent rows. *Watachikan* is a kind of stitch that works on very large motifs and designs and forms

a raised pattern on the fabric. This stitch is used especially for making landscapes. Basically, in this style two kinds of stitches are used—a satin stitch for filling up and a stem stitch for long, continuous linear forms. There is no outlining done in this kind of embroidery. The raised form of the pattern and its shadow form are due to the thickness of the yarn.

5. Apart from shawls, embroidery is done on different costumes such as *choga, achkan,* and *sherwani.* The *Zalakdozi* stitch was the name given to chain stitch embroidery done with a hook on *pherans,* shawls, floor coverings and so forth. The name is derived from a special crochet-like hook used for the embroidery. The hook, known as *Ara Kunj* in Kashmir, resembles the *ari* of Western India or the 'Tambour Needle' of the West. In the beginning of the twentieth century, George Watts had commented that 'Kashmir has within the past twenty years done a large trade with different markets, especially, in the supply of white or variously coloured felt rugs that are more or less richly embroidered by wool in chain stitch.' A range of articles was made, such as, felt *namdasto* (rug), spreads, coverings, dress materials, and curtain cloths.

6. In the early period, pashm wool yarn was used for embroidery work, but later embroidery with *zari* thread was also practised. This is known as *tilladar* in North India. *Tilladar* refers to a work decorated with *tilla,* a metallic thread of gold or silver. Basically, two types of

threads were used: *tilla* and cotton. The decorative *tilla* thread, which remains only on the surface, was tied down over the surface with the help of an additional cotton thread that was yellow or white. There are three different ways in which the *tilla* threads were used: the most common was small loops, which were made by twisting the 'three-ply *zari*'. Each *tilla* loop is stitched down one by one by the cotton thread. A series of loops standing vertically on a base line is common. The next type of *tilla* embroidery is done in a straight line in which the *tilla* is taken along with the design and once again stitched down at short intervals. A series of close parallel lines fill a nearly linear surface. The third is a coil form. The *tilla* is taken in concentric rings starting from the centre and is used to make circles and similar forms. According to Mr Gulam Nabi, a famous embroiderer of the last decade of the last century, Rishi Baf Chikan began this kind of *tilla* embroidery in Kashmir approximately two hundred years ago.

7. When the *amlikar* shawls had come into the industry, new styles were introduced: the *do-rukha* is one of them. The *do-rukha* is the finest achievement of shawl-making in Kashmir and adjacent areas. *Do-rukha* means double-sided or reversible. In this technique, embroidery is done in such a way that the pattern appears the same from both sides. It was woven in panels using the twill tapestry technique. Later, the seamstress worked on it, stitching it to the required shape. Occasionally, the stitching work on panels was done after the embroidery. Finally, a running stitch with a single thread was used to embroider the outline of the motifs. No loose threads were left on the reverse side, resulting in reversible shawls. The reign of Dogra ruler Ranbir Singh (1856-1887) is considered most important for reversible shawls, as many of them were produced then.

8. Next in importance is the *do-ranga* which, literally, means two-coloured. The weaving was done in a manner similar to the *do-rukha*: a coloured area or often the whole ground of a side of the shawl was covered by a different coloured yarn of pashm using a couching stitch. The beauty of these stitches is that they follow the direction of weave and imitate perfectly the 'ribs' of the shawl twill. Contrasting colours between the front and the back of the shawl seldom appear in this technique.

It took many days or even months for the selection of the pattern and for tracing and doing embroidery by using different stitches. Before the piece was sent to the market, it was washed gently with cold water.

WORLD FAMOUS SHAWLS

Raised work on fabric always gives a fine effect, which is true in the context of Kashmiri embroidery, especially, when it resulted in some unparalleled examples in the history of Kashmiri shawls. A few worth mentioning are the 'Sikandarnama shawl', 'Map shawls' and the 'Victory shawls'.

During the time of Gulab Singh of Jammu (1846-69), the famous *Sikandarnama* shawl was created. Today, it is the prized possession of the Chandigarh Museum of Art, Punjab. It depicts some of the principal events in the life of Alexander the Great. The entire shawl is embroidered with figures, architectures, flowers and animals. The most important part of this shawl is its big circular colophon in the centre. The calligraphy of the colophon is very good and it is surrounded by twenty small rectangular scenes. The work has all the characteristics of the period such as streamer-like floral cones with bent tips, almond tree motifs and costumes that reflect the influence of Persian art.

The most momentous of the Map shawls were four shawls with a map of the Kashmir valley, which give a bird's eye view of Srinagar, the capital of Kashmir. Two are in the Victoria and Albert Museum, London; one is in the National Gallery of Australia, Canberra; and one is in the Sri Pratap Singh Museum, Srinagar. Combining cartography with elements of Indian painting, they highlighted Mughal architecture and drew densely constructed Srinagar stretching along both banks of the Jhelum. Mountains, rivers, lakes, palaces, and people all were embroidered. These fine shawls were made on royal commissions during the reign of Maharaja Ranbir Singh (1875 – 1885).

Noted traveller G.T. Vigne in his *Travels in Kashmir* says, Maharaja Ranjeet Singh of Punjab had commissioned a pair of shawls illustrating his victory procession. But it is unfortunate that nothing is known about these shawls. 'Sikargarh' and 'Ramza Nama' are two other themes with lots of figured designs.

Although these are only a few known examples of famous Kashmiri embroidery, in literature there are several examples of such workmanship. Well known Indo-Persian poetical romances such as the *Khamsa of Nizami* and *Iyar-i-Danish* of Abul Fazl inspired the artists of the early nineteenth century to illustrate animal and human figures via various mediums and embroidery was one such medium. These references show that around the middle of the nineteenth century several magnificent woollen shawls and spreads were made on order.

The *amlikar* shawl gave workers an opportunity to select the subject and the working space. The most fashionable items were created by breaking the barriers of loom limitation, shawl sizes, and standard themes. The selection of the workplace was the primary gain for the artisan. While working on *kanikar* shawls, workers were supposed to work in the *karkhanadar*'s place, that is, at the *karkhanas* only and the conditions of some *karkhanas* was not good. While working on *amlikar*, however, they generally preferred to take work home from the master embroiderer.

Kashmiri embroidery also saw men and women working together, which is not the case with other Indian embroidery traditions.

The biggest advantage of *amli* work was the creative freedom of the artisans. As compared to the *kani* cloth, woven on the set norms of the loom, *amli* has a bigger area to work on. Since the making of the bigger *rumal*, several shawl cloths were made individually, which were stitched together either before or after the embroidery. The standard-size shawl was soon replaced by the larger *do-shalla*, spread and *rumal*. Apart from creating the floral patterns of the *kani* weave, *amlikar* shawl-makers had plenty of designs. Different stitches were adopted for doing embroidery and some extraordinary objects were created, which were beyond the imagination of *kani* shawl weavers.

HANDKERCHIEFS AND SPREADS

After the Kashmiri shawl and sash, the most popular is the *rumal* or handkerchief. These *rumals* are bigger than the usual *rumal*, therefore, they could have been used as spreads. These colourfully embroidered *rumals* were used as gift wraps, table covers, and book wrappers. According to G. Watts, 'They are very possibly an evolution from the handkerchiefs that were and are still made in Kashmir, Chamba, and Kullu and are probably more ancient than the Mohammadan conquest of Kashmir.' Such kerchiefs were popular in exhibitions organised by the British at Jaipur in 1887 and 1889 and at Delhi in 1903. They have heavily embroidered borders, *kalka botehs* in the corner, and a plain or intricately embroidered centre field. It is significant that these patterns are frequently ornamented with animal figures and mythological scenes. This shows they may have a Hindu origin.

FACING PAGE: DETAIL OF GULAB SINGH'S SIKANDARNAMA SHAWL, KASHMIR, PASHMINA, MID-19TH CENTURY

107

FACING PAGE & ABOVE: MAP SHAWL, 19TH CENTURY, KASHMIR, PASHMINA, WOVEN AND EMBROIDERED.

Since Indians preferred to sit on the floor in houses, palaces or courts the artisans made different floor spreads—a tradition followed by Mughal and later rulers. Many woollen floor spreads were made with fine stitches and good colour combinations on spreads, *rumals,* and shawls around the nineteenth century. Such fine embroidered fabrics made by using woollen or *zari* thread were the hallmark of articles in Kashmir and adjacent areas. The few most popular are shawls, *patkas,* (sash) *rumals* (square spreads), table clothes, *dastarkhans* (spreads used as dining mats), *jajams* (long, rectangular spreads used for floor covering) and other spreads. According to pattern, Kashmiri embroidery can be divided into two distinct groups: the first contains motifs with mainly floral patterns; the second has patterns of humans, birds, and animal figures plus floral patterns. It appears that in the early stage of shawl making, floral patterns were embroidered with a Persian effect. In the later stages, under the influence of non-Muslim rulers and Europeans, figurative work was done.

109

110

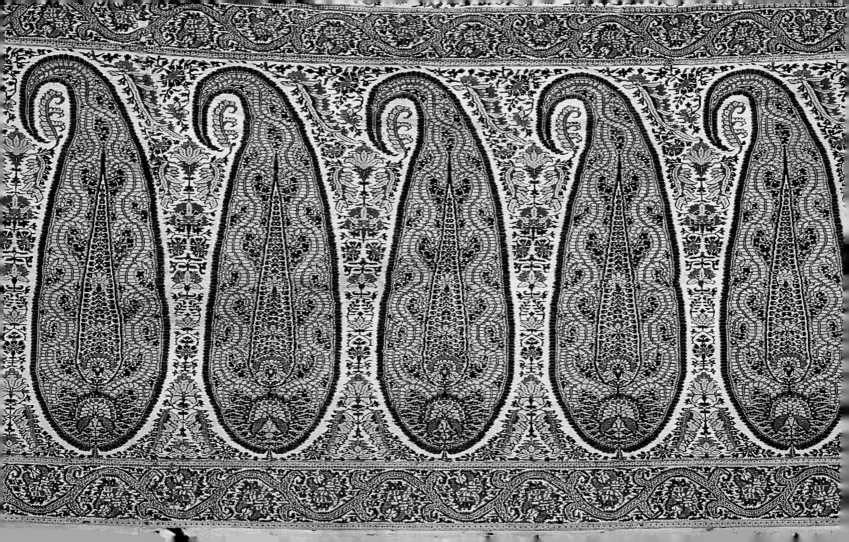

A rare shawl

SHAWL, KASHMIR, LATE 19TH CENTURY, PASHMINA, WOVEN AND EMBROIDERED
COLOUR: (B.G.) OFF-WHITE, (P) MAROON, BLUE, YELLOW
SIZE: 314.6 x 129.6 CM

This long pashmina shawl is a rare example of having similar *boteh* patterns, the centre motif, in *kani* and *amli* work in similar fashion. The broad end panel and side border of the shawl is elaborately and colourfully woven, illustrating the pointed curved tip on the left side of the *kalka boteh*. An intricately designed floral pattern and a creeper are woven between the two *botehs*. The most interesting part of the shawl is the depiction of a similar *kalka boteh* embroidered on the corner. It is surrounded by a floral pattern worked in the shape of a *kalka boteh* and adds balance to the *kani* work. The horizontal and vertical *hashias* depict the floral creeper pattern. The *Amli kalka* corner *boteh* is done so minutely that from a distance it gives the impression of a weave.

113

The garden motif

RUMAL / SPREAD, PASHMINA, EMBROIDERED, KASHMIR, EARLY 19TH CENTURY
COLOUR: RED (B.G.), YELLOW, BLACK, GREEN, WHITE, PINK, RED (P)
STITCHES: SUZANI, STEM, DARN; SIZE: 188 X 180 CM

Mughal rulers, who missed the gardens and the natural surroundings of their motherland, were always inspired to create the same in different art forms, especially, in miniature paintings and textiles. So, one can see the garden motif in pile carpets, printed cotton *quants*, and woollen embroidered spreads of Mughal-period textiles. This maroon red woollen *rumal* / spread is a beautiful example of the continuity of that Mughal tradition although this piece belongs to the early nineteenth century. The entire surface is magnificently embroidered with a variety of stitches such as *suzani*, satin and stem stitches in yellow, pink and white woollen threads. The entire field is minutely embroidered with intricate patterns illustrating the stylised floral creeper, hooked vine motif and tiny flowers. These flowers are arranged in a star-like formation in the centre. The corner of the field forms attractive floral creepers and stylised *botehs*. A beautiful broad border done in a pattern similar to the one on the field and fringe gates illustrate stylised floral *botehs*. The garden effect is well reflected in this colourful spread.

The new-look spread

PASHMINA, KASHMIR, LAST QUARTER OF THE 19TH CENTURY
COLOUR: MAROON, RED (B.G.), YELLOW, GREEN, BLUE, PINK, BLACK (P)
STITCHES: SUZANI, SATIN, STEM; SIZE: 192 x 176.5 CM

Around the last quarter of the nineteenth century, new features were added to *amlikar* work probably due to the influence of Hindu rulers and market demand. This *rumal* is a fine example of this group, where human, bird and animal figures dominate the embroidery. The centre field of this spread, which is surmounted by three types of borders, is decorated in a four-petal flower design. One composition has a couple sitting in a house boat / pavilion as the central theme and corner decoration of the spread. The adjacent area has been left plain and the sides are intricately embroidered with a floral creeper. Three minutely embroidered borders are the beauty of the spread. The most intricate border is the centre one, while the other two are narrow and depict only floral and zigzag patterns. A very attractive centre border has human figures: a royal person with an attendant, a lady on a chair, a rider. These are done in alternate big and small, arched and compartmentalised divisions. The females wear *langha choli* and *odhani* and males wear a tunic skirt, full-sleeved jacket, and turban. Such *rumals* were popular in the early nineteenth century and were probably created for the European market.

The semi-circular shawl

PASHMINA, EMBROIDERED, SRINAGAR, KASHMIR, 1870
COLOUR: OFF WHITE (B.G.); RED, MAROON (P)

A semi-circular shawl with a beautifully ornamented field, which is further surrounded with borders and fringes, is a rare example of late nineteenth-century work. Generally, Kashmiri shawl weavers made rectangular or square shawls, but this semi-circular shawl is charming and was probably made on order as a cloak. The entire field of this off-white shawl is fully embroidered with small floral *buties*. The corner depicts two elongated *kalka buties* done in pine-tree shape and the centre depicts a semi-circular motif that is surmounted by a canopy or *chattra*. Fine embroidery, an unusual shape, excellent colour balance and beautiful small floral motifs make this shawl an especially designed piece perhaps made for the European market.

The red sash

PASHMINA, WOVEN AND EMBROIDERED, KASHMIR, EARLY 19TH CENTURY
COLOUR: RED (B.G.), BLUE, YELLOW, GREEN, WHITE (P)

The woollen *patka* is beautifully embroidered with big *kalka botehs* having a pointed curved tip on the right side and on the end panel while the field is plain. Flowers are arranged in the *kalka boteh,* and between the *boteh* several figures are shown: women sitting on a throne under a pavilion, musicians, musical instruments, men in conversation and horse riders. The entire space between the *boteh* is fully embroidered with a procession of horses, elephant riders, bullock carts, musicians, dancers and lots of animals. All figures have been done so finely that this sash may have been made on order.

The red jajam

PASHMINA, EMBROIDERED, KASHMIR, MID-19TH CENTURY
COLOUR: RED (B.G.), BLUE, MAROON, PINK, GREEN, YELLOW, BLACK (P)
STITCHES: SUZANI, CHAIN, DARN, STEM, FILLING; SIZE: 440 x 117 CM

Spreads of different sizes were used to decorate the floors of the court and the palace, the throne and even the dinning space during the nineteenth century. The square spreads were most popular, but occasionally rectangular spreads were made only to decorate the passage or the throne. This rectangular, brilliant red woollen spread known as *jajam* was probably used to decorate the passage or the floor of the palace and is an excellent example. The *jajam*'s entire centre field is embroidered with seven big floral *botehs* arranged in a row with the intricately embroidered borders adding to the beauty. These floral *botehs* are in a garden-type arrangement, so that each one is surrounded by slightly smaller *botehs* on the four corners. These *botehs* illustrate *kalka* patterns, tiny flowers and floral creepers arranged in the star formation. These remind one of the *alpana* (auspicious floor decorations done with rice paste) motifs of Bengal. The remaining area is filled with floral creepers, depicting different flowers and a colourful crescent motif. The border depicts lots of *kalka boteh* pairs in different sizes, the tree, hooked vine, leaf, and tiny flower motifs. The outer-most edge has a narrow border depicting the floral creeper in chain stitches. The garden-like composition, fine embroidery, colour contrast make this *jajam* a good nineteenth-century example.

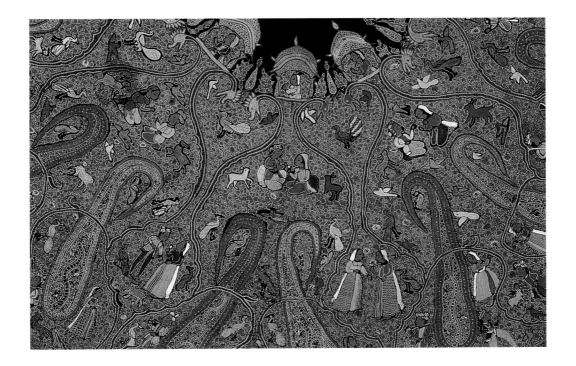

The circle of figures

SQUARE SPREAD, PASHMINA, EMBROIDERED, KASHMIR, MID-19TH CENTURY
COLOUR: BLACK (B.G.); YELLOW, BLUE, WHITE, PINK, GREEN, ORANGE, BLACK (P)
STITCHES: SUZANI, CHAIN, STEM; SIZE: 152 x 147 CM

Figurative representation in a circle within a square spread, of Persian influence, is a popular style of Kashmiri embroidery. This small black square spread is embroidered with plants and animals within a circular frame surrounded by a small border. The centre portion of the spread is plain and eight *shikara* / pavilions are arranged in a circle; the remaining field is decorated with plants and animals of Kashmir. At the bottom of these *shikara* are a pair of long snakes which are in ogee arches and woven all over the spread. The ogee pattern makes several small divisions, each with different scenes: a couple conversing, ladies in conversation, men playing with animals, standing lady, a soldier, birds and animals. Most of the female figures are in *lehangas*, full-sleeved *cholis* and *odhanis*, the men wear pyjamas or trousers, full-sleeved coats or jackets and turbans. The narrow border illustrates a pair of horses, sheep, a ram, peacock, crane and snake. This is the most common variety of spread decoration often found in a single square panel. Sometimes four such panels are stitched together to make a bigger spread.

The floor spread

DETAIL OF FLOOR SPREAD, PASHMINA,
KASHMIR, EMBROIDERED, 19TH
CENTURY
COLOUR: BLACK (B.G.), WHITE,
PINK, YELLOW (P)

A similar kind of flora and fauna is
found in this black pashmina floor
spread. The details of the spread
illustrate animals, bird figurines
while the remaining field depicts
colourful floral creepers.

124

The floral do-rukha

PASHMINA, KASHMIR, DOGRA PERIOD,
LAST QUARTER OF 19TH CENTURY
COLOUR: BROWN (B.G.); BLUE, MAUVE, GREEN, PINK,
MAROON, YELLOW, MUSTARD, WHITE (P)
STITCH: DARN, STEM; SIZE: 332 x 145 CM (F)

The *do-rukha* has double-sided embroidery done on the woven pattern of the shawl. This is the finest achievement of Kashmiri embroidery. The uniformity of repeated floral patterns all over the field, the small border, fringes and fringe gate are the salient features of this mauve and mustard *do-rukha*. The entire shawl field is decorated with the ogee arch pattern. The ogee arch is done in a meandering form and each arch is decorated with compact stylised *boteh* illustrating the lotus, rose, lily, leaves and buds. The most interesting feature of this shawl is the small portion around the *boteh* and the ogee arches that have been left plain. This works like an outer frame and adds beauty to the patterns—probably a European influence. Three borders and a fringe gate are around the centre field of the shawl. The centre border illustrates the three-flower motif surrounded by tiny flowers. Both the surrounding narrow borders depict the floral creeper. Long fringe gates are brown and blue alternately and the dividing lines are in green and orange. These gates depict the arches at the top. A small *boteh* is embroidered while the remaining area is left plain. This beautifully balances the colours.

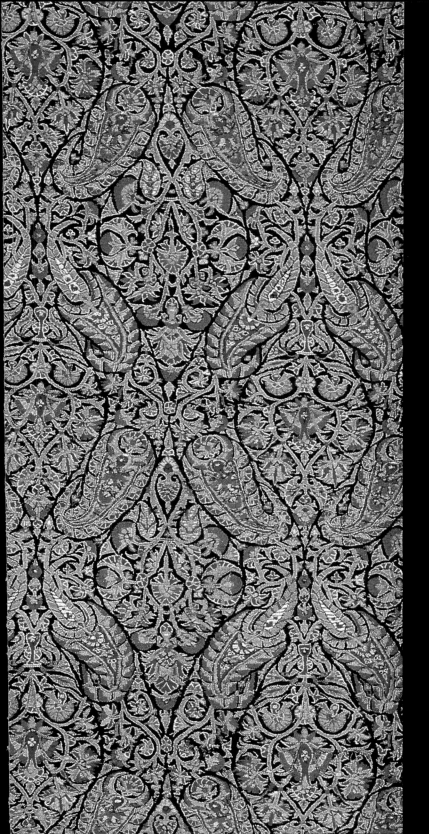

The black do-rukha

DORUKHA SHAWL, PASHMINA, EMBROIDERED, KASHMIR,
DOGRA PERIOD, LAST QUARTER OF 19TH CENTURY
COLOUR: BLACK (B.G.); GREEN, YELLOW, MAROON, PINK,
WHITE, BLUE (P)
STITCH: SUZANI, DARN, STEM
SIZE: 310 x 132 CM

This black shawl is also a good example of an ogee pattern done like a *dorukha*. The variation of the pattern has *kalka* motifs arranged in an ogee arch frame in a stylised form. The ogee arch depicts small flower motifs arranged artistically while the plain un-worked surface portion all around the *boteh* and ogee frame becomes a part of design and appears to be an outline for the motif. An additional horizontal border depicts a stylised, arched pattern that looks like a decorated hanging. *Kalka* motifs are arranged in an ogee arch frame in a stylised form. An additional horizontal border depicted a pattern. Then, a little calligraphy was embroidered in a chain stitch near the end.

The chinar pattern do-rukha

SHAWL, PASHMINA, EMBROIDERED, KASHMIR, DOGRA PERIOD, LAST QUARTER OF 19TH CENTURY
COLOUR: PEACH, OFF-WHITE (B.G.); MAROON, GREEN, BROWN, PINK, BLUE, GREEN, YELLOW, BLACK (P)
STITCHES: SUZANI, DARN, STEM; SIZE: 232 x 116 CM

The *chinar* leaf pattern is a pattern that has been used often by the artists of Kashmir in metal ware, papier-mâché or textiles. This shawl is woven and embroidered in peach and off-white and illustrates the *chinar* pattern all over the field in different colours. Colour contrast in weave and embroidery is the beauty of this shawl. The colourful, woven border of the shawl depicts unfinished embroidery—an illustration of how much embroidery adds to beauty. This shawl may have originally had a small vertical *hashia* that depicts floral *buties* in a foliage pattern. The end panel, an additional horizontal *hashia*, vertical *hashias* and fringe gates appear to be later additions. The end panel depicts an arched compartment that has *botehs* beginning from the flower vase and the *kangri* posh flower; rose and radial-type decorations fill the *botehs*. Long, vertical, multicolour stripes form the fringe gates at the end. They are embroidered with tiny flowers and arched gates. The *do-rukha* shawls have fineness, sophistication and beauty.

130

The red tablecloth

Pashmina and zari, embroidered, Punjab, mid-19th century
Colour: red (b.g.); yellow (p)
Stitches: Looped and spiral; Size: 120 x 120 cm

Zari on pashmina cloth became popular in northern India, and such shawls were made for occasional wear or as gifts. Apart from the shawl, tablecloths and covers were also made. This small square red tablecloth is a good example of early *zari* embroidery illustrating a garden-like formation in which all eight directions lead to the central platform. It illustrates circular decorative motifs which lead to *kalka botehs* in four directions. Between the corner *botehs,* one *kalka* pattern placed on a triangular mound is beautiful. One border has a small flower and *kalka buties* all around. A fringe gate decorated with small floral *buties* adds to the beauty of the tablecloth.

Intricate zari shawl

Shawl, pashmina and zari, Embroidered,
Punjab, mid-19th century
Colour: red (b.g.); yellow (p)
Stitches: Looped and spiral
Size: 260 x 133 cm

Around the late nineteenth century, *zari* embroidery was so intricate that the ground of the fabric could not be seen. Such work was probably a replacement for *kalabatu* work. This plain pashmina shawl is elaborately embroidered on the end panel. It has a plain red field, elaborate *zari*-embroidered end panels, stylised corner *kalka botehs* and horizontal and vertical *hashias*. Intricately embroidered end panels depict the overlapping of a pair of *kalka botehs*. The *botehs* are filled by the pine motif and smaller *buties*. The architectural arches are prominently done on the upper portion and between the *kalka botehs*. An additional border illustrates a row of *kalka boteh*; the crescent and flower motifs are between the end panels and corners. A nice, thin brocade border is on the vertical edge. Prominently embroidered flower *botehs* are on the compartmentalised and arched fringe gate. A small portion has been left plain. This balances the plain field and makes the *zari* embroidered end panel very beautiful.

ZARI EMBROIDERY, BACK OF CHOGA, 20TH CENTURY,
KASHMIR / PUNJAB, PASHMINA.

Shawl with intricate embroidery

PASHMINA, SILVER AND GOLDEN ZARI, EMBROIDERED, PUNJAB, LATE 19TH CENTURY
COLOUR: RED, GREEN, MAROON, BLUE, YELLOW AND BLACK ALTERNATELY
STITCHES: LOOPED, SPIRAL, TILA WORK; SIZE: 280 x 124 CM

The ground surface of the pashmina is embroidered so intricately that it becomes difficult to distinguish the colour of the background. The *Ganga-Yamuni* work on the long shawl leads to the use of silver and gold threads running in vertical stripes all over the field on a background of different colours. Six coloured vertical stripes are arranged alternately over the field. They illustrate the *kalka boteh*, zigzag, ogee and floral motifs in a repetitive manner. Both *hashias* depict smaller *kalka buties* and the pine tree motif with *zari* thread. Nice fringe gates decorated with circular flower *buties* are at the edge. This kind of *zari* shawl is of later-period workmanship, generally used by courtiers in court or on some occasional function.

These simple, *do-rukha* or *do-ranga amlikar* shawls, square, rectangular or semi-circular shawls, spreads, handkerchiefs, and other woollen fabrics demonstrate the special art of the Kashmiri embroiderers. Though embroidery on wool is carried out in Punjab, Himachal, and adjacent areas, the Valley has something special in terms of the composition of design, the colours used and artistic sophistication.

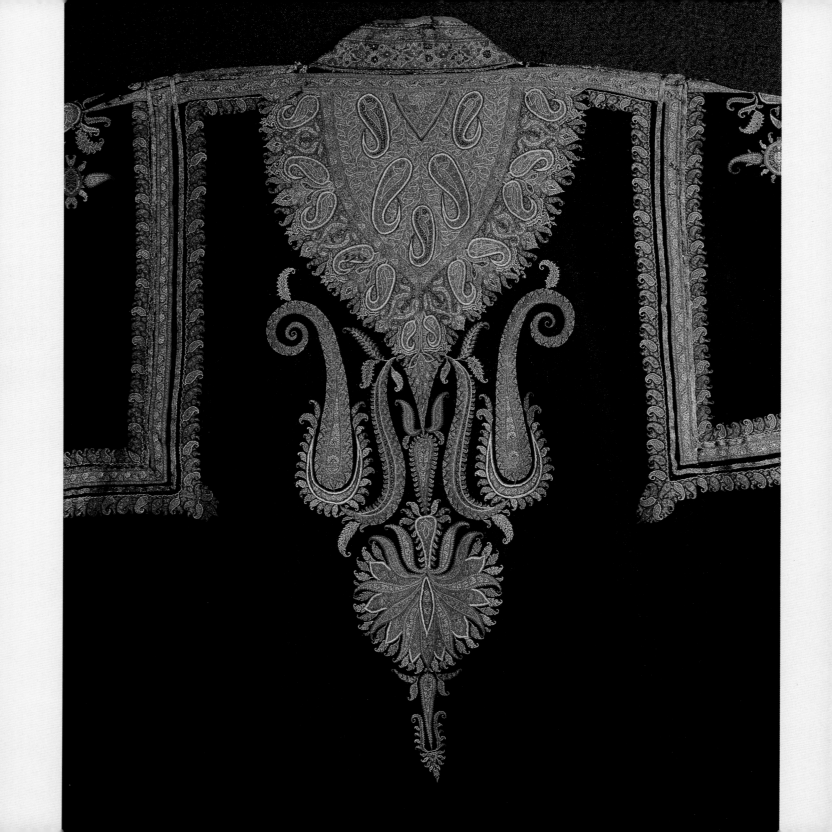

APPENDIX:
WOOLLEN COSTUMES & JAMAWAR

The beauty of Indian costumes lies in its richness of weaving, use of brilliant colours and skilful patterning. Most objects of the eighteenth-nineteenth century are in collections. Much indirect information appears in ancient and medieval literature and visual evidence is found in stone, metal and wooden sculptures, frescoes and paintings on walls, palms, wood, cloth and paper. All these references give ample examples of different costumes used at different times. The most important and vivid picture comes from numerous Mughal miniature paintings from the sixteenth century.

India has rich cotton, silk and woollen costumes, but it is difficult to detail all types. Here only woollen costumes, especially of Kashmir will be discussed. These costumes are rich in technique, diversified in fashion and full of colour and pattern. Since the sixteenth century, the Mughals, Afghans, Sikhs and Dogras ruled Kashmir; their influence is noticeable.

Different types of wool are used for making woollen costumes. They are decorated with patterns on loom while the plain woven ones are embellished with embroidery. The shawl cloth or pashmina fabric is woven in different sizes as related in early texts. One such important text is the *Ain-i-Akbari*, which covers shawl making in detail, but gives less information about woollen costumes. It informs that

BACK OF CHOGA, KASHMIR, LATE 19TH CENTURY, PASHMINA, EMBROIDERED.
FACING PAGE: BACK VIEW OF WOOLLEN CHOGA, 19TH CENTURY, KASHMIR, WOVEN AND EMBROIDERED.

137

'His Majesty (Akbar) improved the width of all stuff, [and] had the pieces made large enough to yield the making of [a] full dress.' The eighteenth-nineteenth century costumes can be divided into two groups according to their popularity and utility: the *choga, sherwani, achkan, jama* and *pheran* belong to the main group while the coat, cloak, long skirt, pyjama and cap are in the other.

Most Kashmiris wore traditional woollen costumes for different occasions. The difference among these costumes lies in their ornamentation. Woven garments with patterns were used for daily wear, while *zari*-embroidered ones were kept for formal occasions. These costumes reflect the influence of Kashmiri shawls.

The *choga, sherwani, achkan* and *jama* were upper garments used by men in court as is known from literary and visual references of the sixteenth century and after. The *choga* (a Turkish term) is a long, loose-fitting outer garment. Males wore *chogas* over their *jamas* or *angrakhas*; apparently, the *choga* was an Afghan dress. These were made of a soft woollen material and embroidered with woollen or *zari* threads. The most attractive part of the *choga* were the *kalka buties* and leaf patterns that were embroidered in rich colours on the borders of the sleeves and shoulders. Occasionally, the embroidery would extend to the back.

The *sherwani* is a buttoned, knee length, coat-like garment. The *achkan* is a close-fitting, long-sleeved coat buttoned to the waist and reaches down to the knees. *Achkans* and *sherwanis* were court costumes. They were made of woven pashmina and had shawl-like patterns. These patterns often illustrate the floral creeper, *kalka buti,* flower or folio designs. The cutting and stitching was done as these costumes were being tailored, so as to avoid spoiling the pattern.

The upper half of the *jama* was high-waisted and fit snugly over the chest. The *jama* was knee length with a flared skirt, tied under the right or the left armpit

DETAIL OF EMBROIDERED CHOGA, KASHMIR, 19TH CENTURY, PASHMINA.
FACING PAGE: DETAIL OF EMBROIDERED CHOGA, KASHMIR, 19TH CENTURY, PASHMINA.

with cords. Although *jamas* were usually of cotton or brocade, occasionally woollen ones were made. The *pheran* is a long, loose-fitting, closed outer garment with a small opening for the neck. The *pheran* is also embroidered with pashm wool or *zari* thread.

Jamawars

The literal meaning of *jamawar* is 'grown piece', the technical and trade name for a shawl cloth or long shawl. Such pieces are woven on loom, have an intricate pattern, and can be used as dress material for *chogas*, *achkans*, *sherwanis*, gowns, jackets or shawls.

The most significant reference to the *jamawar* also comes in the *Ain-i-Akbari* (see page 137) but it does not say anything regarding the designs of these *jamawars* and the visual evidence from Akbar's period, does not tell much. The next important reference is Moorcroft's. He says, 'The length of this cloth is three-quarter *gaz* and the breadth one-and-a-half *gaz* and these were specially made for the Persian and Afghani markets.'

It appears from literary references that initially the *jamawar* was the trade name for a special kind of woollen fabric that was prevalent among Afghans and Persians. Later, other communities also wore it. It became so popular that weavers started using the term *jamawar* even for those long shawls that had floral designs over the field and did not have any border. These *jamawars* were made of pashm wool though some cotton or silk fibres were also used at times.

The pattern ran lengthwise over the field of the fabric and at times so completely covered the breadth that it ended with fringes resembling the Scotch plaid. The ends were either woven straight from the textiles or woven separately and stitched on later.

Just like the development of shawl, *jamawars* might have gone through different changes in raw materials, designs, and size, as different costumes were made from different widths of dress material. The *jama* and *choga* required different sizes of material—a fact easily noticed in miniature paintings. The same thing has been mentioned in *Ain-i-Akbari* too. The famous *chakdar jama* of Akbar needs lots of yeildage as compared to later period *jamas* or *sherwanis*. These changes occurred due to the choices of the patron as well as the foreign traders. The latter usually came with their designs and often asked weavers to work according to them. Such *jamawar* were popular in India and in Afghanistan, Turkistan, Bokhara, Russia, Armenia, Persia, Turkey and Europe.

The tapestry technique was used throughout for weaving *jamawars*. Such shawls or shawl clothes no longer illustrated simple *boteh* on the end panels; the pattern was repeated all over the field. Sometimes the *boteh* developed an underlying symbolism and played a secondary role. Briefly, the *jamawar* tapestry shawl had and has several elements such as various borders, woven panels, and embroidered fringes. The most striking feature is the floral design of small repeated patterns or stripes on the entire field. Some of the earliest designs that appeared on the *jamawar* are stripes over the field. In fact, it is sometimes affirmed that the *jamawars* are those textiles that have 'woollen textiles with striped designs'.

These are the same textiles that the French are said to have taken to imitating in their striped muslins. It may seem that many designs in the Kashmir *jamawars* were inspired by the designs of the French agents who came for trade, but it would be more likely for the designs to be original. Since these were mainly used for trade, the influence of Persian, Turkish, or European designers can be noticed on these shawls. According to Moorcroft's long list of trade fabrics, there are an infinite number of designs met with in the *jamawars*, but he describes only three. The main two are *rega-buta* or *rezabutha* and *kirkh-buties* or *khukha-butha*. *Rega-buta* involves small flower motifs while *kirkh-buties* had large flower motifs. The third involves *jaldars*, patterns that assume a net-like form.

All these motifs were a repeat of the patterns described in literature and noticed in the eighteenth-nineteenth century miniature paintings and costumes.

GLOSSARY

Amli: embroidery or an embroidered shawl from Kashmir, especially that which became popular around the middle of the nineteenth century.

Bent-tip strawberry: expression for a popular rose-type flower, which gives the impression of a strawberry with its tip bent downwards.

Buta or *Boteh*: hindi term often used for a large flower motif.

Buti: hindi term used for a smaller flower motif.

Coif boteh: a *boteh* whose arching top is highlighted by a detached raceme.

Dhoor: a running pattern that surrounds the *matan* and is close to the *hashia* or border of the *pallu*, especially of the long *do-shalla*.

Do-shalla: the term used for a long woven shawl.

Do-ranga: a *do-rukha* whose ground colour on one side differs from the other; intricate couching stitches make this possible.

Fool's cap: a floral motif of the Sikh period. The pattern resembles a clown or fool's hat, although it looks like a *jigeh*, a jewelled ornament or pin worn in front of turbans by Indian and Persian nobles.

Fringe gates: the different coloured bands of wool at the edge of the shawl and close to the fringe. They are often embroidered with *mehrabs* or arches. Fringe gates began around the mid-nineteenth century.

Hashia: the narrow lateral borders that run the length of the shawl; their patterns are composed of a floral meander.

Ideogram root: this expression is often used for a seventeenth-century Mughal style *boteh*'s root, which appears to be inspired by Chinese ideograms.

Jacquard Loom: in 1805, Joseph Marie Jacquard, a French man, invented the loom, which was named after him. The loom is composed of hooked needles and spring-loaded pins which enmeshed with each of the successive pre-programmed punched cards to form the fabric's pattern.

Jamawar: a trade name for a dress material or gown piece often found in old records. Later, the term was used for a long, decorative shawl.

Kani: means 'woven'. The twill tapestry weave is done with interlocked wefts.

Karkhana: in Mughal texts, the workshops where the shawls were woven.

Karkhanadar: proprietor of a weaving factory.

Khatraaz: a striped pattern that appeared in shawls or other fabrics, which became popular in the middle of the nineteenth century.

Matan: the plain central field of the shawl or *patka*.

Moon shawl: square shawl containing a central medallion and quarter medallion at each corner of the field.

Narikunjara: the motif in which female figures were conjoined in the form of an elephant.

Paisley: term used for *Kalka* or *Kalgha* pattern. Paisley is also a name of a town near Glasgow, Scotland, where imitation Kashmir shawls were made in large numbers.

Pashm: goat's fleece, one of the three main types of wool.

Pashmina: fabric woven with goat fleece.

Patchwork shawl: shawls of the late nineteenth century, made of many separately woven pieces joined together by the *rafugar*.

Patka: sash or waistband. A very long Kashmiri shawl that is narrow in width and can be wrapped around the waist two or three times.

Radial flowers: flowers whose petals or buds are arranged in a precise, circular fashion around the central axis. The style developed in the third quarter of the eighteenth century under the Afghans.

Rafle: one of the three main types of wool used for making shawls. Machine-spun wool comes from merino sheep.

Rafugar: A shawl tailor or seamster.

Rezkar: Executed in multicoloured threads and broad stitches.

Rumal: a square shawl or spread, which was used for different purposes.

Shah-tus or *tus:* one of the three main wool types. Literally, means king's wool. The fleece comes from the ibex, a wild Himalayan mountain goat of the genus *capra* that grazes at very high altitudes. This fleece is rare and the most expensive in the world.

Shikarga: a pattern depicting a hunting scene with different types of animals, hunters, etc. that appeared in the nineteenth-century shawl.

Shuttle: Wooden bobbin with pointed ends that slide back and forth across the loom to insert the weft.

Selvedges: very narrow, sometimes strengthened, strips of un-patterned weave at the sides of a shawl or piece of cloth.

Twill tapestry: a technique by which the decorative wefts pattern is formed by small bobbins of yarns creating areas of colour, the edges of adjacent sections interlocking around the same warp.

Warp: the yarns that are stretched on the loom to form the underlying structure of the cloth.

Weft: the yarn which crosses the cloth at right angles to that in which it was woven; the thread which forms the pattern.

Watchikan: Raised floral designs.

Winged leaf *buti:* a type of small *buti*, its stem supports a lateral projection of a serrated leaf or flower or both. It is usually seen on later eighteenth-century shawls patterned with a trellis chevron, or checkerboard design.

Zari: a twisted metal (gold or silver) thread winded on silken thread.

Zalakdozi: term used for chain-stitch embroidery done with a hook.

BIBLIOGRAPHY

ORIGINAL SOURCES

Ain-i-Akbari, Abul Fazal, tr. Blochmum, ed. S.L.Goomer, 2nd edition, New Delhi, 1965.

Acaranga Sutra.

Amarkosha, Amara Sinha, Bombay, 1890.

Atharva Veda, Pt. Damodar Satvalakar, Pardi, 1958.

Ashtdhyayisutrapatha, Varanasi, 1977.

Brhadaranyaka Upanishad.

Cullavagga.

Gazetteer of Kashmir & Ladak, Delhi, (reprint), 1974.

Gilgit texts, III, 2.

Kautilya's Arthashastra, Kangle, R.P., Bombay, 1963, Part II.

Mahabharata.

Mahabhashya, Patanjali, 1,2,69.

Mahavanija Jataka.

Mahavastu.

Manusmrti, Vidyalankar, Pt. Harish Candra, Delhi, 1959.

Nisithacurni, Litho ed., Vol VII.

Pietro della Valle, Vol II.

Rig Veda.

Ramayana of Valmiki.

Sasa Jataka.

Satapatha Brahmana, tr. Eggeling, J., Part III., reprint, 1963, Delhi.

Sivi Jataka.

Sukayjurveda Samhita, tr. Upadaya, Pt. Ganga Prasad, Delhi, 1922.

Taittiriya Samhita.

The Imperial Gazetteer on India, The Indian Empire, Oxford, 1908, Vol 3.

Vessantra Jataka.

Yajur Veda.

Desopadesa, ed. Kaul, M., Poona.

Moorcroft, MSS, Eur. E113.

Narmamala, Kaul, M.

Tuzak-i-Jahangiri, II.

Kalpadrukosa, ed. Sharma, R., Baroda, 1923.

SECONDARY SOURCES

Agnes, G., *A History of Textile Art*, London, 1979.

Agrawala, V.S., *India as known to Panini*, Varanasi, 1963.

Ahad, A., *Kashmir to Frankfurt*, Delhi, 1987.

Anavian, R.G., *Royal Persian and Kashmir Brocade*, Kyoto, 1975.

Ames, F., *Kashmir Shawls*, England, 1986.

Baker, A.F., *Cottage Textile Industries of Kashmir and their Prospective Development*, England, 1933.

Balfour, E., *Encyclopedia Asiatica*, VIII, New Delhi, 1976, reprint, 1844.

Bamzai, P.N.K., *Socio-Economic History of Kashmir*, Delhi, 1987.

Beal, S., *Si-Yu-Ki, Buddhist Records of the Western World, Translation from the Chinese of Hiuen Tsiang (A.D. 629)*, London, 1908.

Bernier Francois, *Travels of the Mughal Empire, 1656-1668*, London, 1891.

Brand, M., and Glenn D. Lowry, *Fatehpur Sikri: A Sourcebook*, Cambridge, 1985.

Brand, M., *The Vision of Kings*, Australia, 1995.

Cunningham, A., *Ladak, Physical, Statistical and Historical with notices of the surrounding countries*, (reprint), New Delhi, 1970.

Chakraverty, A., *Indian Miniature Painting*, Delhi, 1996.

Coomaraswamy, A.K., *Yakas*, Delhi, 1980.

Das, S., 'Cashmere,' in *Fabric Art: Heritage of India*, Delhi, 1992.

Desai, V. N., *Life at Courts*, Boston, 1985-86.

Dongerkery, K.S., *Romance of Indian Embroidery*, Bombay, 1951.

Eden, Emily, *Up the Country, Letters from India*, London, 1978.

Balfour, E., *Encyclopaedia Asiatica*, VIII, New Delhi, 1976.

Fane, H. E., *Five Years in India*, London, 1842, Vol.I.

Forster, G., *A Journey from Bengal to England,* I, London, 1798.

Gattinger, M., *Master Dyers of the World*, Washington D.C., 1982.

Goswamy, B.N., *Piety and Splendour*, Delhi, 2000.

Gulati, A.N., *Source Book of India Archaeology*, ed. Allchin and Chakravarti Dilip, Delhi, 1997.

Irwin, J., *Shawls: A study in Indo-European influences*, London, 1955, reprinted as *The Kashmir Shawl*, London, 1973
————, *Embroidered Textiles*, Ahmedabad.

Jain, J., and A. Agrawal, *National Handicrafts and Handlooms Museum*, Ahmedabad, 1989.

Janet, R., 'Woven Textiles,' *Crafts of Jammu, Kashmir and Ladakh*, ed. J. Jaitly, Ahmedabad, 1990.

Kenoyer, J. M., *Ancient Cities of the Indus Valley Civilization*, Oxford, 1998.

Khanna, P., *Embroidered Crafts of Kashmir*, Ahmedabad, 1992.

Makey, *Indus Valley Civilization*, Calcutta, 1931.

Mukhtar, S. H., 'A Treatise on the Art of Shawl Weaving,' Lahore, 1887, tr. Ahmad Dar Bashir, Srinagar, 1981.

Moorcroft, W., Travels in Hindustan: *Himalayan Provinces of Hindustan and Punjab in Ladak and Kashmir in Peshawar, Kabul, Kunduz and Bokhara*, Vol.II, 1971.

————, 'A Journey to Lake Manasarovara in Un.Das a Provenince of Little Tibet,' *Asiatick Researches*, XII, Calcutta.

Moorcroft, W., and G. Treeck, *Travels in the Hindustan Provinces of Hindustan and Punjab; in Ladakh and Kashmir, in Peshawar, Kabul, Kunduz and Bokhara*, London, 1841.

Neelam, and G. Amarjeet, *The Needle Lore,* Delhi, 1988.

Qsborne, W.G., *The court and camp of Ranjeet Singh*, London, 1840.

Pal, P., *Romance of the Taj Mahal*, Delhi, 1989.

Parks, F., *Wanderings of a Pilgrim in Search of the Picturesque*, Karachi, 1975.

Powell, B.H.B., *Handbook of the Manufacturers and Arts of the Punjab,* II, Lahore, 1872.

Raychaudhuri, T., and I. Habib, ed. *The Cambridge Economic History of India*, Vol I.

Robert, Skelton, 'The Indian Heritage,' exhibition catalogue, Festival of India, Britain, 1982.

Rosemarry, Crill, 'Textiles in the Punjab,' *The Arts of the Sikh Kingdoms*, ed. Strong S., London, 1999.

Saraf, D.N., *Arts and Crafts of Jammu and Kashmir*, Delhi, 1987.

Sarkar, J., *The India of Aurangzeb,* Calcutta, 1901.
————, *Mughal Administration*, Delhi.

Singh, C., and D. Ahivasi, *Woollen textiles and costumes from Bharat Kala Bhavan*, Varanasi, 1981.

Sircar, D.C., *Select Inscription*, Vol I, Calcutta, 1965.

Smart, E., and D. Walker, *Pride of the Princes*, USA, 1985.

Srinivasacharya, L., *Gautam Dharma Sutra with Maskari Bhashya*, Mysore, 1917.

Strauss, M.L., *Romance of the Cashmere Shawl*, Ahmedabad, 1986.

Strong, S., *The Arts of Sikh Kingdom*, London, 1999

Suryakanta, *A Practical Vedic Dictionary*, Suryakanth, Delhi, 1981.

Sushil, Wakhlu, 'Embroidery,' *Crafts of Kashmir, Jammu and Ladakh*, ed. J. Jaitley, New York, 1990.

Turner, S.M., *Ambassade au Thibetat au Boutan*, translated into French by J. Castera, Paris, 1800.

Vigne, G.T., *Travels in Kashmir, Ladak, Iskardo and the countries adjoining the mountain course of the Indus and the Himalaya, North of the Punjab*, London, 1842.
————, *Travels in Kashmir*, 2 vols, London, 1842, reprinted in New Delhi, 1981.

Watts, G., *Indian Art at Delhi 1903*, Calcutta, 1903.
————, *A Dictionary of Economic Products of India*, VI, Part II, Delhi, 1972.

Welch, S.C., *India: Art and Culture*, New York, 1986.